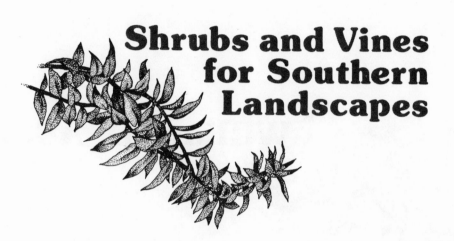

Shrubs and Vines for Southern Landscapes

William D. Adams

Shrubs and Vines for Southern Landscapes

Pacesetter Press
A Division of Gulf Publishing Company
Houston, Texas

Illustrated by
Terry J. Moore

Shrubs and Vines for Southern Landscapes

Library of Congress Catalog Card Number 76-15455

ISBN 0-88415-804-7

Edited by B.J. Lowe
Designed by Leigh McWhorter

Contents

Southern Shrubs and Vines: What They Are, What They Offer, 1

What Is a Shrub?, 1; Southern Shrubs and Vines: Their Uses and Features, 3

How to Care for Your Shrubs, 6

How to Transplant Shrubs, 6; Planting Bare-Root Shrubs, 6; Planting B & B or Canned Nursery Stock, 6; Fertilizing Shrubs and Vines, 7; Mulching, 8; Pruning, 9; Herbicides, 11; Insects, 11; Diseases, 15

A Guide to Southern Shrubs, 17

A Guide to Southern Vines, 51

Other Shrubs for the South, 59

Other Vines for the South, 63

A Spacing Guide to Southern Shrubs and Vines, 65

Index, 67

of special interest...

Hardiness Zone Map

This map shows in moderate detail the expected minimum winter temperatures in the areas comprising the South. Although this book is applicable to the areas within the bold outline, every gardener should check with his or her local agricultural Extension agent for information on variety selection and availability, and special cultural practices necessary for the particular area.

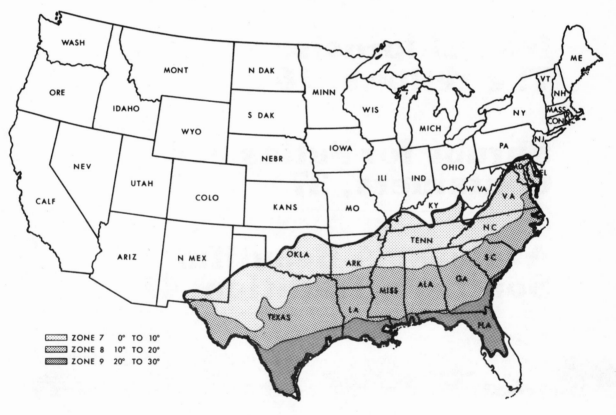

ZONE 7   0° TO 10°
ZONE 8   10° TO 20°
ZONE 9   20° TO 30°

Climate Data for Southern Cities

	Last Spring Freeze	First Fall Freeze	Frost-Free Days	Record January Low (°F)	Minimum Hours of Chilling	Inches of Rain
Alabama						
Birmingham ..	Mar. 19	Nov. 14	241	1	1,000	53
Huntsville	Apr. 1	Nov. 8	221	−9	1,100	50
Mobile	Feb. 17	Dec. 12	298	14	500	67
Montgomery ..	Feb. 27	Dec. 3	279	5	700	51
Arkansas						
Little Rock	Mar. 16	Nov. 15	244	−4	1,000	49
Florida						
Jacksonville ...	Feb. 6	Dec. 16	313	2	400	53
Orlando	Jan. 31	Dec. 17	319	24	300	51
Tampa	Jan. 10	Dec. 26	349	23	200	51
Georgia						
Atlanta	Mar. 20	Nov. 19	244	−3	800	49
Macon	Mar. 14	Nov. 7	240	3	700	44
Savannah	Feb. 21	Dec. 9	291	9	500	48
Kentucky						
Lexington	Apr. 13	Oct. 28	198	−15	1,400	43
Louisville	Apr. 1	Nov. 7	220	−20	1,400	41
Louisiana						
Baton Rouge ..	Feb. 28	Nov. 30	275	10	500	55
New Orleans ..	Feb. 13	Dec. 9	300	14	400	64
Maryland						
Baltimore	Mar. 26	Nov. 19	238	−7	1,400	43
Mississippi						
Jackson	Mar. 10	Nov. 13	248	7	700	50
North Carolina						
Charlotte	Mar. 21	Nov. 15	239	4	900	43
Greensboro	Mar. 24	Nov. 16	237	0	1,100	43
Oklahoma						
Oklahoma City	Mar. 28	Nov. 7	223	0	1,200	32
Tulsa	Mar. 31	Nov. 2	216	−2	1,300	38
South Carolina						
Charleston	Feb. 19	Dec. 10	294	11	600	49
Columbia	Mar. 14	Nov. 21	252	5	700	47
Tennessee						
Knoxville	Mar. 31	Nov. 6	220	−16	1,100	45
Memphis	Mar. 20	Nov. 12	237	−8	1,000	49
Nashville	Mar. 28	Nov. 7	224	−6	1,100	47
Texas						
Austin	Mar. 15	Nov. 20	244	12	700	33
Dallas-						
Ft. Worth ...	Mar. 18	Nov. 17	244	5	1,000	33
Houston	Feb. 10	Dec. 8	301	19	600	44
San Antonio ...	Feb. 24	Dec. 3	282	0	600	26
Virginia						
Norfolk	Apr. 4	Nov. 9	219	10	1,100	44
Richmond	Apr. 20	Oct. 18	181	−12	1,200	44

Horticultural Consultants

Alabama

David Bradford, Extension Horticulturist, Alabama Cooperative Extension Service, Birmingham

Arkansas

Gerald Klingman, Extension Horticulturist, Arkansas Cooperative Extension Service, Fayetteville

Georgia

Troy Keeble, Extension Horticulturist, Georgia Cooperative Extension Service, Atlanta

Louisiana

Severn Doughty, Area Horticulturist, Louisiana Cooperative Extension Service, Metairie

Tom Pope, Extension Horticulturist, Louisiana Cooperative Extension Service, Baton Rouge

Mississippi

James T. Garrett, Leader, Extension Horticulture, Mississippi State University, Mississippi State

North Carolina

Arnold and Connie Krochmal, Agriculture and Science Associates, Asheville

Oklahoma

Raymond Kays, Extension Horticulturist, Oklahoma Cooperative Extension Service, Stillwater

Texas

William D. Adams, Extension Horticulturist, Texas Agricultural Extension Service, Houston

Neal Sperry, Professional Horticulturist, Dallas-Ft. Worth

Terry A. Wilbourn, Extension Horticulturist, Texas Texas Agricultural Extension Service, San Antonio

Southern Shrubs and Vines: What They Are, What They Offer

A tremendous number of shrubs and vines are available for use in southern landscapes, but since the primary wholesale production areas for these plants are California and some of the southeastern states like Louisiana, Alabama and Florida, varieties of shrubs adapted to those states predominate while a great many shrubs *native* to other southern states remain little used or undiscovered and undeveloped.

Fortunately, most shrubs and vines lend themselves to asexual propagation (in the form of cuttings) more readily than trees do. This greatly simplifies the production of large numbers of selected specimens. And since this is so much easier, very few shrubs and vines are grown from seed.

What Is a Shrub?

A shrub is often defined as a multi-trunk, woody plant 20 feet or less in height. While this description will suffice in most instances, any definition of this kind is an attempt, at best, and is of limited validity. Many shrubs can be trained to make interesting small specimen trees simply by reducing the number of trunks and by pruning the lower branches to expose the form of these trunks. An excellent example is the shrub, xylosma. Normally used as an evergreen shrub, it can be pruned to three or four trunks, and if these trunks are trimmed up, xylosma makes an unusual and very attractive small evergreen tree for the landscape or in a large container.

Conversely, there are also some small trees which are often grown as shrubs—sumac, for example.

What is a shrub? That depends on the plant and the way you train it. This xylosma, usually a medium-sized evergreen shrub, has been meticulously pruned to a single trunk, making it a fine tree-like specimen.

Traditionally, shrubs are used up close to the house, usually to hide the less attractive features of the foundation, utilities, etc . . .

. . . But why not get them out in the yard, where they can create a natural, wooded effect?

These shrub/trees will initially require diligent pruning to remove sprouts which may pop up at the base of the tree and along the stems. These plants become "shrubs" when more than four trunks are allowed to develop and when these trunks are hidden by foliage from the ground up.

Shrubs are often considered as plants to use around the house to hide the foundation. This was one of their earliest uses, but because unsightly foundations are less common in today's homes, it's not necessary to limit the use of shrubs to this type of a planting scheme. In today's landscape, shrubs often work better when used to frame other plantings, or when used in mass to create a natural thicket appearance. Shrubs have as many uses as you can dream up; perhaps the most notable use is as a screen for privacy.

Shrubs have many and varied characteristics, too: fragrance, flowers, ornamental fruits, shape, foliage color, cultural requirements, etc. Choosing just the right shrub for the right place in your southern landscape may not be easy, but it certainly is a challenging and interesting opportunity. Though the following list of shrubs, based on characteristics and uses, is by no means complete, you should find it a useful beginning guide.

Southern Shrubs and Vines: Their Uses and Features

Shrubs That Can Be Trained as Small Trees

Camellia sasanqua (Sasanqua Camellia)
Elaeagnus multiflorus (Gumi)
Feijoa sellowiana (Pineapple Guava)
Ilex decidua (Deciduous Holly)
Ilex vomitoria (Yaupon) *illustrated*
Lagerstroemia indica (Dwarf Crapemyrtle)
Ligustrum japonicum (Japanese Ligustrum)
Photinia species (Photinia)
Sophora secundiflora (Mescal Bean Sophora)
Xylosma senticosa (Shiny Xylosma)

Shrubs For Screening

*Impenetrable because of thorns
**Dense growth

Abelia grandiflora (Abelia)
Elaeagnus pungens (Elaeagnus)
Feijoa sellowiana (Pineapple Guava)
Ilex cassine (Dahoon Holly)
Ilex vomitoria (Yaupon)
Jasminum mesnyi (Primrose Jasmine)
Ligustrum lucidum (Glossy Privet)
Nerium oleander (Oleander)
Photinia species (Photinia)
Pittosporum tobira (Pittosporum) *illustrated*
Poncirus trifoliata (Trifoliate Orange)*
Prunus caroliana (Cherry Laurel)
Prunus laurocerasus (English Laurel)
Viburnum japonicum (Japanese Viburnum)**
Viburnum odoratissimum (Sweet Viburnum)**
Viburnum suspensum (Sandankwa Viburnum)
Viburnum tinus robustum (Roundleaf Viburnum)
Xylosma senticosa (Shiny Xylosma)*

Flowering Shrubs

Abelia grandiflora (Abelia)
Brunfelsi pauciflora (Yesterday-Today-and-Tomorrow)
  illustrated

Camellia japonica (Japanese Camellia)
Camellia sasanqua (Sasanqua Camellia)
Cassia corymbosa (Flowery Senna)
Chaenomeles japonica (Flowering Quince)
Forsythia species (Forsythia)
Gardenia jasminoides (Gardenia, Cape Jasmine)
Hydrangea macrophylla (Hydrangea)
Hypericum species
Jasminum floridanum (Italian Jasmine)
Jasminum mesnyi (Primrose Jasmine)
Nerium oleander (Oleander)
Philadelphus virginalis (Mock Orange)
Punica granatum (Pomegranate)
Pyracantha species (Fire Thorn)
Raphiolepis indica (Indian Hawthorn)
Rhododendron (azalea) species (Azalea)
Sophora secundiflora (Mescal Bean Sophora)
Spirea species (Spirea)
Viburnum suspensum (Sandankwa Viburnum)
Viburnum tinus robustum (Roundleaf Viburnum)

Shrubs with Fall Color

Itea virginica (Virginia Sweetspire)—red *illustrated*
Nandina domestica (Nandina, Heavenly Bamboo)—red
Rhus copallina (Sumac)—red
Vaccinium arboreum (Tree Huckleberry, Farkleberry)
  —red

Shrubs with Gray Foliage Color

Cotoneaster glaucophylla (Grayleaf Cotoneaster)
Cotoneaster pannosa (Silverleaf Cotoneaster)
Elaeagnus pungens (Thorny Elaeagnus)
Feijoa sellowiana (Pineapple Guava)
Leucophyllum frutescens (Ceniza—Texas Purple Sage)
Mahonia trifoliolata (Agarita) *illustrated*

Shrubs with Fragrant Flowers

Calycanthus floridus (Carolina Allspice)
Elaeagnus pungens (Thorny Elaeagnus)
Gardenia jasminoides (Gardenia, Cape Jasmine)
Itea virginica (Virginia Sweetspire)
Mahonia trifoliolata (Agarita)
Osmanthus fragrans (Sweet Olive)
Philadelphus virginalis (Mock Orange)
Pittosporum tobira (Pittosporum)
Sophora secundiflora (Texas Mountain Laurel, Mescal Bean Sophora) *illustrated*
Viburnum odoratissimum (Sweet Viburnum)
Viburnum suspensum (Sandankwa Viburnum)
Vitex agnus-castus (Lilac Chaste-tree)

Shrubs with Fragrant Foliage

Calycanthus floridus (Carolina Allspice)
Laurus Nobilis (True Laurel) *illustrated*
Lindera benzoin (Spicebush)
Myrica cerifera (Southern Waxmyrtle, Bayberry)
Myrtus communis (Myrtle)
Vitex agnus-castus (Lilac Chaste-tree)

Shrubs with Spring Color on New Foliage

Abelia grandiflora (Abelia)—bronze *illustrated*
Cleyera japonica (Cleyera)—reddish-bronze
Photinia species (Photinia)—red
Xylosma senticosa (Shiny Xylosma)—bronze

Shrubs for Wet Soil

Aronia arbutifolia (Red Chokeberry)
Calycanthus floridus (Carolina Allspice)
Clethra alnifolia (Summer-sweet)
Ilex cassine (Dahoon [Cassine] Holly)
Ilex glabra (Inkberry)
Ilex vomitoria (Yaupon)
Itea virginica (Virginia Sweetspire)
Leucothoe populifolia (Leucothoe) *illustrated*

Lindera benzoin (Spicebush)
Myrica cerifera (Southern Waxmyrtle)

Shrubs for Dry Soil

(Most like a neutral or slightly alkaline pH, 7.0 and above)

Elaeagnus pungens (Silverthorn)
Ilex vomitoria (Yaupon)
Leucophyllum frutescens (Ceniza, Texas Purple Sage)
Mahonia trifoliolata (Agarita)
Nerium oleander (Oleander) *illustrated*
Punica granatum (Pomegranate)
Sophora secundiflora (Mescal Bean Sophora, Texas Mountain Laurel)

Shrubs Which Require an Acid Soil

Camellia japonica (Camellia)
Camellia sasanqua (Sasanqua)
Gardenia jasminoides (Cape Jasmine)
Ilex cassine (Dahoon Holly)
Itea virginica (Virginia Sweetspire)
Leucothoe populifolia (Leucothoe)
Rhododendron species (Azalea) *illustrated*
Vaccinium arboreum (Farkleberry)
Vaccinium ashei (Rabbiteye Blueberry)

Shrubs Which Grow Well In the Shade

(*Partial shade)

Aralia seiboldii (Fatsia)
Aucuba japonica (Gold Dust Plant) *illustrated*
Camellia japonica (Camellia)
Camellia sasanqua (Sasanqua)
Cleyera japonica (Cleyera)*
Gardenia jasminoides (Cape Jasmine)
Ilex cassine (Dahoon Holly)*
Ilex cornuta (Chinese Holly)*
Ilex vomitoria (Yaupon Holly)*
Leucothoe populifolia (Leucothoe)
Mahonia bealei (Leatherleaf Mahonia)
Myrtus communis (True Myrtle)
Osmanthus fragrans (Sweet Olive)
Rhododendron species (Azalea)*

Flowering Vines

Bignonia capreolata (Cross Vine)—yellow, cinnamon brown

Bougainvillea x Buttiana (Bougainvillea)—pink, purple, yellow, red

Clematis sp. (Clematis)—red, also white, blue, purple, yellow

Gelsemium sempervirens (Carolina Yellow Jessamine)—yellow

Antigonon leptopus (Coral Vine)—pink, white

Campsis radicans (Trumpet Vine)—orange, reddish orange, coral, yellow

Lonicera sp. (Honeysuckle)—red, yellow, white

Macfadyena [Doxantha] Unguis-cati (Cat's Claw)—yellow

Passiflora caerulea (Passionflower)—blue

Rosa banksiae (Banksia Rose)—yellow, white

Senecio confusus (Mexican Flame Vine)—orange

Stigmaphyllon ciliatum (Butterfly Vine)—yellow *illustrated*

Thunbergia alata (Black-eyed Susan Vine)—orange, white

Trachelospermum jasminoides (Confederate Jasmine)—white

Wisteria sp. (Wisteria)—lavender, white, purple

Fragrant Vines

Bignonia capreolata (Cross Vine)

Gelsemium sempervirens (Carolina Yellow Jessamine)

Lonicera japonica (Japanese Honeysuckle)

Trachelospermum jasminoides (Confederate Jasmine)

Wisteria sinensis (Wisteria) *illustrated*

Evergreen Vines
(*Semi-evergreen)

Bignonia capreolata (Cross Vine)*

Bougainvillea x Buttiana (Bougainvillea)

Clematis texensis (Texas Clematis)*

Ficus pumila (Climbing Fig)

Gelsemium sempervirens (Carolina Yellow Jessamine)*

Hedera canariensis (Algerian Ivy) *illustrated*

Hedera helix (English Ivy)

Lonicera sp. (Honeysuckle)

Macfadyena [Doxantha] Unguis-cati (Cat's Claw)*

Trachelospermum jasminoides (Confederate Jasmine)

Wisteria milletia (Evergreen Wisteria)

Vines for Wet Soils

Antigonon leptopus (Coral Vine)

Campsis radicans (Trumpet Vine)

Dioscorea bulbifera (Air Potato) *illustrated*

Gelsemium sempervirens (Carolina Yellow Jessamine)

Lonicera japonica (Japanese Honeysuckle)

Trachelospermum jasminoides (Confederate Jasmine)

Vines for Dry Soils

Bougainvillea x Buttiana (Bougainvillea)

Campsis radicans (Trumpet Vine) *illustrated*

Clematis texensis (Texas Clematis)

Ficus pumila (Climbing Fig)

Lonicera sempervirens (Trumpet Honeysuckle)

Senecio confusus (Mexican Flame Vine)

Vines for Shade or Partial Shade

Bignonia capreolata (Cross Vine)

Clematis sp. (Clematis)

Dioscorea bulbifera (Air Potato)—also sun

Ficus pumila (Climbing Fig)—also sun

Gelsemium sempervirens (Carolina Yellow Jessamine)—blooms more abundantly in partial shade or sun

Hedera canariensis (Algerian Ivy)

Hedera helix (English Ivy)

Lonicera sp. (Honeysuckle)—also sun

Trachelospermum jasminoides (Confederate Jasmine)—blooms more abundantly in partial shade or sun *illustrated*

How to Care for Your Shrubs

How To Transplant Shrubs

Planting Bare-Root Shrubs

When planting bare-root shrubs, dig a hole large enough to allow the root system to spread naturally . It is not necessary to dig the hole much larger. Check the root-packing material to make sure it is moist, and don't allow the roots to dry out. If you plan to plant within the next few hours, soak the roots in a pail of water during this time. If it will be several days before you plant, dig a shallow trench and "heel in" the plants.

Before planting, cut back any broken or damaged roots. Mound good topsoil in the bottom of the hole to form a cone on which to spread the root system. Backfill the hole three-fourths full, working the soil firmly around the root system with your fingers to eliminate air pockets. Fill the hole with water and let settle. This should eliminate any remaining air pockets. Finally, add the remaining topsoil. Unless the topsoil is very deep, it may be advantageous to add organic matter, about one-third by volume, to the soil used as backfill. Watering can be facilitated by creating a watering basin with the extra soil mix. In areas of high rainfall and poor drainage, the watering basin may cause more problems that it is worth.

Planting B & B or Canned Nursery Stock

Balled and burlapped shrubs, as well as those grown in containers, have an advantage over bare-root shrubs in that their root systems are relatively undisturbed. So avoid breaking or damaging the root ball to get the best performance from B & B trees. Most nursery stock of this type can be planted any time of the year.

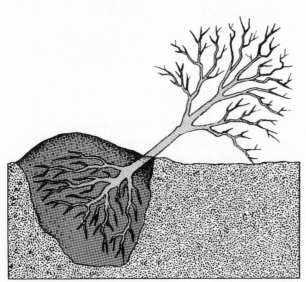

If it will be several days before you can plant your bareroot shrub, heel-in the transplant with moist soil to prevent the roots from drying out.

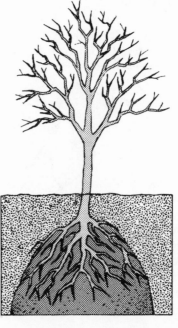

Before planting, mound good topsoil in the bottom of the planting hole to form a cone on which to spread the root system.

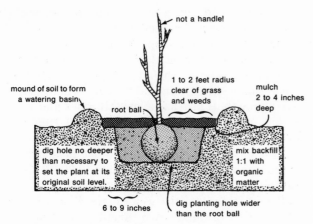

Planting, in sandy, well-drained soils or in areas of low rainfall.

Planting in clay or poorly-drained soils in areas of high rainfall.

Occasionally you may buy a shrub that has been growing in a container too long and has become root-bound. This condition is characterized by a mass of roots spiraled around the bottom and sides of the container and usually growing out of the drainage holes. In addition, the plant usually appears stunted.

Begin by thoroughly soaking the root ball. Let it stand several hours in a pan of water or completely immerse it for about 15 minutes. Unless you pry and loosen this root mass or cut some roots, the plant will probably never outgrow this condition. If you have to damage or remove part of the root system, you will need to compensate by pruning off about one-third of the top growth.

Dig the hole no deeper than is necessary to set the plant at its original soil level or slightly higher (1 to 2 inches) and 12 to 18 inches wider than the root ball. When planting in a sandy soil, save the topsoil and mix it 1:1 with organic matter such as peat moss, pine bark or compost. Utilize this mixture to backfill the hole.

If the soil is a tight clay, backfill with the original clay topsoil. Organic matter may be mixed in, but in areas with high rainfall and poor drainage, reserve this mixture for the final ⅓ of the backfill. Firm the soil but do not pack it, especially if it's tight clay.

With the hole ¾ full, water thoroughly to settle the soil around the roots. A root starter (high-phosphorus fertilizer such as 0-20-0) may be used but it is not absolutely necessary. Newly developed "slow-release" planting tablets are also safe to use and supply fertilizer for several years.

In an area with as many variations in soil conditions, climate and topography as the South, it is difficult to give general instructions without men-tioning exceptions. Some of these are described below.

Time of Year:
Summer—may need watering basin, even along the Gulf Coast.
Winter—knock down any watering basin if season is rainy and drainage is poor.

Type of Plant:
Some plants, such as southern wax myrtle and other wetland species, will tolerate poor drainage. Others, such as azaleas, require special planting techniques.

Topography:
If plants are on a definite slope, drainage is not a problem even with tight soil and high rainfall.

Climate:
Areas of low rainfall definitely need a watering basing plus the addition of more organic matter to help hold moisture. This is particularly true where this condition is combined with poor soil.

Fertilizing Shrubs and Vines

There are a number of speciality fertilizers listed as "Tree and Shrub foods" or as azalea/camellia fertilizers. Special fertilizers for azaleas are offered because these plants require acid soil. Such fertilizers generally contain cottonseed meal and an acidifying nitrogen source such as ammonium sulfate. These fertilizers are fine for feeding shrubs.

Complete fertilizers such as 12-24-12, 12-12-12, or 13-13-13 can also be used to fertilize shrubs. Use

¼ cup per plant if the shrub is more than 1 year old but less than 3, and ½ cup per plant for older plants. The fertilizer should be applied near the drip zone of the shrub (the outer edge of the leaves), and it should be lightly scratched into the soil with a rake. After you apply the fertilizer, water it in.

The best time to fertilize is in early spring (March-April) and again in May or June. Azaleas and other spring-flowering plants are often fertilized immediately after blooming.

Fertilizers to Have On Hand

Most home gardeners will find it handy to have the following in 40 to 50 lb. sacks:

1. *Ammonium sulfate (21-0-0):* This is a nitrogen-only fertilizer, a salt-type fertilizer, and is handy for lawn fertilization and other situations where all you need is nitrogen.
2. *Superphosphate (0-20-0):* A phosphorus-only fertilizer handy for making starter solutions and stimulating flower, fruit and seed formation.
3. *Ammonium phosphate (16-20-0):* A nitrogen-and-phosphorus combination for use where these two elements are needed.
4. *Cottonseed meal:* A balanced, organic, slow-release fertilizer with an analysis of 6.5-3.0-1.5, plus all the trace elements.
5. *Ferrous sulfate:* Use only in alkaline soil areas. This is iron sulfate, sometimes called copperas. It contains 20 percent iron in a soluble form available to plants if not tied up by soil reactions.
6. *Dolomite:* This is limestone that also contains magnesium. Helpful in mixing with peatmoss to raise the pH when making up potting soils such as peatlite.
7. *Steiner solution:* This is an 8-5-16 analysis with all the trace elements in proper proportion for feeding patio plants in containers, houseplants, or home greenhouse sand culture. One tradename for this is "Pronto Hydroponic Special," available from Pronto Fertilizer Co., P.O. Drawer 247, Wisner, La. 71219.

Starter Solutions

When a plant is transplanted, either bare-root or with a root ball, transplant shock may occur. The reason for this is that the transplant has a limited root system and thus a limited capacity to take up plant foods and water. Adding a starter solution of liquid fertilizer at transplanting time will reduce shock and help the plant get off to a good start.

A starter solution should be rich in phosphorus, since this element stimulates root formation and early growth. It also has a low salt index and won't injure young roots. Another important rule is to keep the solution weak.

Probably the best fertilizer to use in making a starter solution is superphosphate (0-20-0). Use 2 tablespoons of 0-20-0 or 1 tablespoon of 0-46-0 per gallon of water and stir well to mix. Pour 1 gallon of solution around each small transplant at transplanting.

Mulching

Mulches are especially good for shrubs and vines. They help reduce the competition from weeds, and since many plants (like azaleas) require an acid soil, an acid mulch such as pine bark will help maintain the proper soil pH. As the mulch gradually decomposes it realeases acidifying substances which affect the soil.

Many mulching materials are available in the South; pine bark is perhaps the most readily available and decorative. Other good materials are cedar shavings, bark chips, decayed sawdust, pecan shells, bagasse, and pine needles.

Because mulching materials break down so rapidly in the South, it's important to renew them at least annually, and in some areas twice annually.

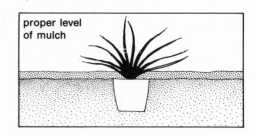

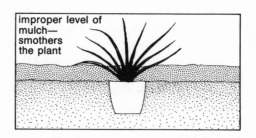

Proper thickness of mulch allows normal development of the plant.

Mulching Materials

As with so many gardening materials, availability of mulches is subject to local variation. If you have a choice, here is some information to help you select one:

Good Choices

Bark. In the South, pine bark is usually readily available and relatively inexpensive. Use the shredded form as it looks the best and doesn't float away as readily as the nuggets (bark chips that are available in various graded sizes). Sometimes pine bark is offered as a "soil conditioner" in a very finely ground form. This is not suitable for mulch, as it tends to be easily blown or washed away. Pine bark is acid in reaction. Add nitrogen to compensate for the amount lost in the decomposition process. Redwood and fir bark chips are also available in various sizes, but are usually more expensive than pine bark. Otherwise, they have the same characteristics as pine nuggets. Apply the various barks to a depth of about three inches.

Bagasse (Sugar cane pulp). This has great water-holding capacity (a potential problem for plants preferring dry soil). It is acid in reaction and slow to decompose. Apply 1 to 2 inches deep.

Leaves. Obviously not commercially available. Leaves from different species of trees have different characteristics when used as a mulch. Some will pack together and exclude air from the soil. These should be stirred occasionally. Don't use them around vines and shallow-rooted shrubs, as you are likely to uproot some plants in the process of stirring. Shredded leaves are best since they do not pack together as much and fit better around small transplants.

Live Oak leaves are acid in reaction and do not pack down. Other types of oak leaves may pack a little more. Maple and elm leaves are alkaline. Maple and poplar leaves tend to pack together. Non-packing or shredded leaves can be applied 2 to 4 inches deep.

Pine Needles (Pine Straw). Of course, these, too, are leaves. They're acid in reaction, slow to decompose, and allow good air and water penetration. Pine needles don't absorb water themselves; they're better when shredded. Potential fire hazard when dry. Apply about 2 to 4 inches deep.

Wood Chips. Available from local tree service companies, often free (particularly from those trimming trees for utility companies). Slow to decompose, coarse and therefore allowing good air and water penetration. Varying in pH depending on the trees included (usually a mixture and therefore hard to know the composition). Add nitrogen to compensate for the amount lost in decomposition. Apply 2 to 3 inches deep.

These Are Not the Best

Plastic. Used effectively in farming but not really suitable for shrubs and vines. In order to allow water to penetrate, holes must be made in the plastic. Weeds come through the holes. When the weeds are pulled, a larger hole is ripped in the plastic, etc., etc., etc. Also, the plastic is very unattractive. If covered with another mulch to improve appearance, the cost gets out of hand. The runners of trailing vines are unable to root in the ground if a plastic mulch is used.

Peat Moss. Good as a soil conditioner (although expensive) but not as good for mulching. It is difficult to wet once it becomes dry, and it tends to cake on the surface, repelling water. Also, when dry, peat moss is flammable and easily blown about by the wind.

Rice Hulls. Another good soil conditioner that does not double as a mulch. The surface dries out rapidly and cakes somewhat. Also, rice hulls are easily blown about by the wind and, being very small, tend to get into a lot of unauthorized places.

Sawdust. The biggest problem with sawdust as a mulch is the fact that it cakes on the surface. When it is loose, it is easily blown by the wind.

Pruning Shrubs

Pruning is a necessary art, one that is very difficult to explain, for no two shrubs are ever alike. Perhaps for this reason pruning is one of the most misunderstood and improperly executed horticultural practices. All too often shrubs are pruned in hedge-like fashion rather than with a specific type of training in mind. The nandina is an outstanding example of a shrub which is often pruned improperly. This can be one of the easiest plants to care for, but it often becomes leggy and unsightly because it gets lopped off waist high with the pruning shears each year. The key to an

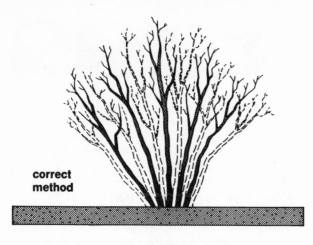

correct method

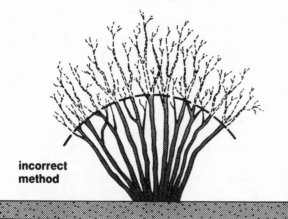

incorrect method

Most shrubs should be pruned by thinning out rather than heading back. When you cut all the tops off, you often produce a gnarled, stunted plant.

flower in the spring, which may be producing buds at the time you plan to do your pruning. Especially notable in this regard are azalea, aronia, camellia, tulip magnolia, banana shrub, mock orange and spirea. These plants should be pruned soon after blooming. Most other shrubs are pruned during the dormant season. Shrubs that are grown simply as big green screens will probably need pruning several times a year, including summer. With summer pruning you don't get as much vigorous regrowth as you do from dormant season pruning.

Don't make pruning too complicated. Try to keep the shrubs' natural growth habits in mind as much as possible (except for formal hedges) and avoid leaving large stubs on the plant. This may be impossible if you're cutting back old ligustrum or pittosporum hedges, but if at all possible try to make cuts where the branches connect to another limb or to the main trunk.

Painting large cut surfaces with pruning paint seems to be of less value than was at one time thought, but if you feel the need to put some coating on cut surfaces, white latex paint should be adequate. The important point is to make an even cut flush with trunk to promote rapid healing.

When transplanting shrubs, some of the root system is often damaged. It's best to prune about 25 percent off the top of the plant to balance things out.

(Text continued on page 12)

attractive nandina plant is to completely remove some of the old canes at the crown of the plant each year, thus causing new shoots to renew from the base. This keeps the plant dense and attractive.

There are many reasons for pruning, the most usual being to keep a plant in bounds. So many of our shrubs rapidly outgrow the small spaces provided for them in the landscape, and soon they hide windows and other architectural features. Dwarf shrubs have partially answered this problem.

Shrubs may also be cut back to remove dead or winter-killed growth, to compensate for loss of root system during transplanting, to remove diseased portions of the plant, to invigorate older plants, to develop a desired form, and to encourage more flower and fruit production.

When should you prune? If you're pruning to remove nuisance growth, do it any time you're ready. However, you can mess up certain plants by pruning at the wrong time; particularly those that

Topiary: Shrubs Alive!

Have you ever seen a row of ducks or elephants used as a border for someone's yard? Not the fake plaster kind . . . but the kind that are alive? Alive, that is, in the sense that shrubs are alive.

This is called "topiary," which is the art of pruning shrubs and small trees into unnatural (but not unhealthy) growth habits. Southern gardeners practice this art commonly when they fashion the so-called "poodle shrub," pruning their plants into various ball-shaped forms.

The classic technique for developing topiary plants was to plant shrubs or small evergreen trees, such as the bay laurel, and over a period of time shape them into ducks, donkeys, elephants, etc. In the South, an easier plant to work with is the waxleaf ligustrum.

In recent years several companies have been offering wire forms in various animal shapes. You can line these shapes with coarse sphagnum moss and fill with a potting soil. Then you plant a vigorous vine, such as fig ivy, to grow in these self-contained forms. This makes the training much simpler, and although regular watering and fertilization are necessary, you don't have to be a very skilled, experienced pruner.

The "poodle tree" is an extremely popular plant form which can be rather expensive when purchased ready-made from the nursery. But it isn't difficult to produce from a standard shrub.

To grow your own, buy a large, mature plant such as a 5-gallon or a balled-and-burlapped ligustrum. To make sure that you don't cut off the wrong branches, tie a red ribbon around the base stems of each section to be poodled. Then simply begin removing branches in between to leave bare portions of the trunk 12 to 18 inches between each ball of plant growth. After the initial limbs are removed, you can use hedge trimmers to cut back the branches and produce a more dense ball-like form from the stems which were saved.

Forms like these are available from a number of sources, and in about as many shapes and sizes as you can imagine. The rooster is actually creeping fig; the goat, Asiatic jasmine. (Courtesy Topiary, Inc., Tampa, Fla.)

A yaupon (Ilex vomitoria) pruned to poodle form.

shaping hedges

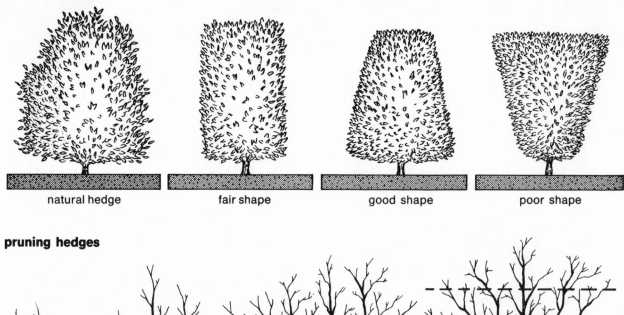

natural hedge   fair shape   good shape   poor shape

pruning hedges

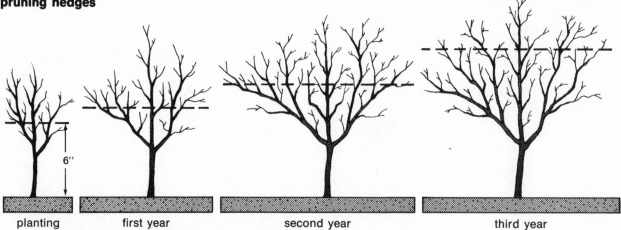

6"

planting   first year   second year   third year

Herbicides Around Shrubs

The use of herbicides in shrub plantings is not nearly as important to the home gardener as it might be to a landscape contractor, but there are still several weed killers that home gardeners can use safely to keep down the amount of weeding to be done. Don't forget mulching! In fact, herbicides are most effective when applied underneath a layer of mulch.

In particular, treflan, dacthal and eptam are generally available in small shaker cans that are easy to apply. For large jobs elaborate equipment and complicated calibration techniques are necessary to ensure accurate application rates.

Another technique used more by the professional landscape contractor is soil sterilization. In this case vapam is a material recommended. Soil sterilization certainly seems attractive where persistent weed pests like nut grass and Bermuda grass may be a problem; unfortunately, vapam is not very effective at controlling nut grass.

Insect And Disease Problems

Many insects and diseases attack and damage shrubs and vines in southern landscapes, and so it helps to select plants that have a minimum of these problems. Any plant that requires periodic spraying to eliminate an insect or disease problem has to have something special to offer in exchange—like camellia blossoms or rose blossoms. The majority of plants in a landscape should be pest-free.

Suggested Insecticides for Pests
in Southern Landscapes

Aphids

Insecticide	Formulation	Amt. to Mix with 1 gal. of Water
diazinon	25% EC	1 tbsp.
dimethoate (Cygon or De-Fend)	2.67 lb. concentrate	1½ tsp.
malathion	50% EC	2 tsp.
	57% EC	1½ tsp.
	25% WP	4 tbsp.
dormant oil	Mix and apply according to directions on the label. Applications should be directed to the trunk and limbs to control the over-wintering eggs and adult forms of woolly, bark and other aphids.	

EC—emulsifiable concentrate
WP—wettable powder

Whiteflies

Insecticide	Formulation	Amt. to Mix with 1 gal. of Water
Diazinon	25% EC	2 tsp.
Dimethoate (Cygon, De-Fend)	2 lbs./gal. EC	2 tsp.
Endosulfan	50% WP	1 tbsp.
Lindane	20% EC	1½ tsp.
Malathion	57% EC	1½ tsp.
Naled	4 lbs./gal. EC	2 tsp.
Acephate (Orthene)	75% WP	2.1 oz.

EC—emulsifiable concentrate
WP—wettable powder

Mites

	Diazinon	Kelthane	Malathion	Sulfur
Shrubs	X	X		X
Bermuda grass	X	X		X
Houseplants		X		
Roses	X	X	X	
Citrus		X		
Marigolds		X		
Pecans	X	X	X	X
Spring-flowering annuals	X	X	X	
Summer-flowering annuals	X	X	X	

Insects

Insects can be classified according to the way they damage plants—by sucking or chewing. Sucking insects do their damage by taking sap away from the plant and often excreting a sticky substance called honeydew which later supports a black, sooty fungus growth. This feeding weakens the plant and the sooty material may further harm it by shading the foliage. Some of the major sucking insects which attack shrubs and vines include:

Aphids (plant lice). These pear-shaped insects seem to attack almost every plant species on earth, but they are worse on some than others. Usually they are relatively easy to control; most general use pesticides will do a good job. Many of them excrete copious quantities of honeydew and are often

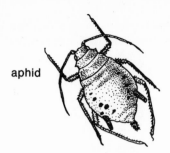

aphid

responsible for the black sooty mold found on the foliage of shrubs and vines. Small populations of aphids are readily controlled by predators like lady bugs; a hard spray of water will knock them off, and it's just too far for them to walk back.

White flies. This insect is becoming one of the most serious pests of southern shurbs, especially on common plants like ligustrum and gardenia. It can be a very persistent and difficult pest to control, and like the aphid, it sucks out its juices and excretes a large amount of honeydew which turns into a black mold.

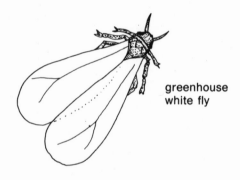

greenhouse
white fly

The creature that does the damage is the immature white fly, which is immobile once it begins to feed on the undersides of the leaves. It looks like a tiny blister. An oil spray is a most effective control for white flies (where it can be used, depending on temperatures and the plant involved). Use a summer oil during warm weather and a dormant oil when temperatures are below 85° and above 40°.The dormant oil is simply a more concentrated dilution of a highly refined oil. These materials suffocate the insects.

Be very cautious with these oils during hot weather, and if in doubt test spray a portion of the plant to be treated. Of course, not all plants will tolerate oil sprays at any season.

Persistence is one of the keys to control of white flies, and once the population is under control, preventing heavy reinfestation is also important. Sprays once every week to two weeks, three spray periods in a row, will probably be necessary to control a heavy infestation.

Mites. The mite is not an insect even though it does similar damage. There are many species, and most suck juices out of plants. One of the worst of all is the two-spotted spider mite, or red spider. It is a persistent pest, one that is difficult to control, with several stages in its life cycle during which it is resistant to pesticides.

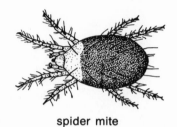

spider mite

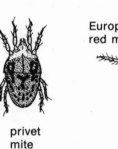

privet
mite

European
red mite

Good control usually requires three sprays at 3 to 7-day intervals with a mitiacide. Spider mites attack a wide variety of plants; in particular they like elaeagnus, pyracantha and they may even attack oaks. Damaged leaves get a stippled appearance, eventually turn yellow or brown, and fine webs may be seen on the undersides of the leaves. The mites are tiny; to see them you may have to use a hand lens, or if you shake plant tissue over a piece of white paper and the dust particles start crawling off, you can be fairly sure that you have a population of spider mites. Some populations of spider mites may be controlled with high-pressure water sprays . . . simply washing them off.

Caterpillars. A number of beetles and caterpillars will chew on shrubs and vines. Most are easily controlled, especially if found while they're still small. Certain caterpillars are of particular concern not because they do such great damage to foliage, but because they may inflict painful stings on humans working around the shrubs. These are the stinging caterpillars, the most common of which is the puss caterpillar, also known as the larva of the flannel moth and incorrectly termed an asp (an asp is technically a snake). They become

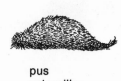

pus
caterpillar

most noticeable in the fall, when they approach maturity and are still only about an inch long. Some persons, after contacting these caterpillars, may require a physician's care and even hospitalization.

IO moth

One other common larva found on shrubs is the IO moth larva, which is a bright green caterpillar with red and yellow stripes lengthwise along the body. It looks like a stinging caterpillar because of many spines on fleshy tubercles. This caterpillar can become quite large—as much as 2½ inches in length—and although the pain of its sting is reportedly less severe, this caterpillar can be quite common. The buck moth larva is similar in size and appearance to the Io moth's but it is a purple-black color with reddish to black tubercles. The saddleback caterpillar, a very unusual caterpillar, is brown with a green spot on its back resembling a saddle blanket.

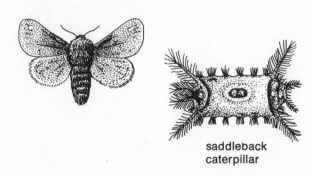

saddleback
caterpillar

The hag moth, another stinging caterpillar, has a number of projections of variable length which have stinging hairs. It is fairly uncommon and the stings of both the saddleback caterpillar and hag moth are reportedly less painful than the others. All of these pests are easily controlled with most pesticides recommended for chewing insects.

Diseases

If diseases are going to be a problem with shrubs and vines in a landscape, the best bet is not to use the plants. The diseases that are most perplexing are those that seem to show up years later; often they're more a symptom of old age than of anything else.

In recent years a great many mature azalea plants have been reported as gradually dying, a few limbs at a time. The limbs first wilt and eventually turn brown; ultimately the entire plant dies. A similar condition has been reported on an old reliable shrub, the pittosporum. In the former case, the disease is apparently a fungal root rot; in the latter case, a fungal stem rot caused by a species in the genus *Pellicularia.* Unfortunately, neither problem has a good control measure. Planting other plants resistant to the disease is probably the best idea.

Some diseases such as petal blight are a nuisance and only require spraying once or twice a year and thus can be tolerated. Specific problems and recommendations for plants are given in the section on individual plants, pages 17-58. Some of the basic problems you can look for are bacterial leaf spot, whose symptoms appear as small dark green or water-soaked spots later becoming brown; fungal leaf spots—brown areas often with tiny dot-sized spore masses; viruses which cause abnormal growth, ring-like spots or mosaic yellow patterns in the leaves.

Diseases that attack stems and branches. Cankers caused by fungi or bacteria result in cracked areas in the bark that may circle the limb and cause death of the limbs affected. Die-back, blackening and death of a stem or branch begins at the tip and progresses downward; this is also caused by fungus or bacteria and various types of galls such as the curious azalea gall which turns leaves thick and fleshy. These galls are often called "Pinkster Apples."

Diseases attacking the root system. In addition to the root rot organisms already referred to, nematodes (small microscopic roundworms) may also damage shrubs; boxwood, in particular, is very susceptible. Using a nematocide is a recommended control, however, many nematocides are no longer available for homeowner use.

Iron Chlorosis: The Yellows

Iron chlorosis is often a problem in alkaline soils, especially with shrubs that grow best under acid conditions. The condition arises when soil pH is too alkaline for roots to absorb the element iron. Plants like azaleas, camellias and gardenias are especially prone. The chlorosis shows up first on the younger leaves because iron isn't readily translocated in the plant. The deficiency is characterized by a loss of green color in the leaves, which turn yellow to almost white between the veins. Though this chlorosis is usually caused by lack of iron, in some instances yellowing can result from poor soil aeration or deficiencies of other elements, such as nitrogen or zinc. These latter symptoms usually show up in other parts of the plant—they're not as localized as iron chlorosis is.

Nematodes are microscopic roundworms that attack the root system. In the process of feeding they weaken the root system and reduce its ability to take up nutrients such as iron. This action may aggravate an iron chlorosis situation, making it show up even worse.

Special preparation of soil beds is required for acid-loving plants like azaleas (see page 47), but supplemental acid can be provided by adding 1 to 2 lbs. of powdered sulfur per 100 square feet. The sulfur needs to be thoroughly mixed with the soil; adding acid organic matter such as peat moss will enhance the effect. Sulfur requires a period of time to work, however, and results will not be immediate.

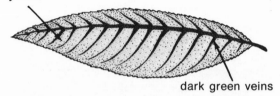

yellow

dark green veins

Iron sulfate (copperas) can be used to correct iron chlorosis, but it's best applied to the foliage; iron chelates can be used either in the soil or on the foliage.

To completely overcome the problem, the soil pH almost always must be lowered by sulfur additions. Once this has been done, the supplemental sources of iron will revive the plants more quickly.

A Guide to Southern Shrubs

Each plant in this section is listed alphabetically by its currently correct botanical name. Immediately below the botanical name is the common name used most widely in the South. Additional common names are given in parentheses. Numbers directly across from each botanical name indicate the height and spread, respectively, of the average mature plant. The zone information below this refers to the northernmost limits of the plants' hardiness, or ability to survive winter freezes (see the map in the front of this book).

Spacing recommendations are included under the heading "Culture." These recommendations are for the standard size of the species, and they are for the average growing season in the South. If you're in a cooler area, space closer; if in a warmer one, space farther. **Spacing recommendations are given in parentheses under the heading "Varieties" if there is a difference in growth habit between the standard species and the listed variety.**

Not all known varieties of each genus and species are listed; those that are known to grow poorly or that are not available in the South have not been included. Special attention is given to native southern species and to species which deserve more attention in southern nurseries and landscapes.

Abelia x grandiflora   **4-8' x 3-6'**
Glossy Abelia   **Zone 6**

Evergreen to semi-deciduous woody shrub of the honeysuckle family (Caprifoliaceae).

Characteristics. Though often trained as a sheared hedge, abelia makes a very attractive oval-shaped shrub if left to grow without training. The foliage has a bronzy tint from spring to fall. The young stems have a graceful arching habit of growth. Flowers are pinkish-white to white, trumpet-shaped, ½-¾ inch long in clusters at the ends of branches, lightly fragrant, not showy from a distance but good up close, summer and early fall. After the flowers fall, pink sepals remain and are almost as attractive if not more so than the flowers.

Culture. Grown in most soils, and although it will tolerate drought, it responds to regular moisture and fertility. Blooming is best in sun but the plant will grow in partial shade. If pruned regularly or sheared, it will continue to flower since flowers are produced on new growth. No significant insect or disease problems. Plant 3 feet apart.

Glossy abelia.

Remarks. Abelia is used more in its northern range than it is in the South, but it deserves increased attention. One possible reason for this slighting is that it becomes partially deciduous even in warm areas, and where a dense evergreen shrub is required, it may look sick during the winter. Though used as a hedge, this plant is perhaps best as a shrub in an informal planting.

Varieties. Edward Goucher, a medium-sized shrub with pink flowers (2-3 feet).

Aucuba japonica   **8′ x 5′**
Japanese Aucuba (Gold-dust Aucuba)   **Zone 8**

Evergreen shrub of the Cornaceae family.

Characteristics. Upright, coarse-textured shrub prized for its ability to grow in shade. Some varieties are grown for attractive red berries. Leaves are 6-8 inches long, ovate or oblong, coarsely toothed and glossy.

Culture. Can be grown in zone 7 in a protected location on the south side of the house or in an interior of a courtyard. It is primarily used as a shade-loving plant to give a tropical appearance. It is best planted in a well drained soil which has had large amounts of organic matter mixed with it. A fungal leaf spot often disfigures the leaves with dark blackened areas, and a general-purpose fungicide applied during late spring and early summer should help to prevent this. Sun scalding may also be a problem where plants are placed in a southerly or southwesterly exposure. Sucking insects cause a black sooty mold by feeding on the shrubs or from honeydew they excrete when feeding on trees overhead. This makes the plants less attractive. Insect control with a general-

Japanese aucuba.

purpose insecticide is necessary to eliminate the source of honeydew. The sooty mold does not directly attack the plants. Plant 30 inches apart.

Remarks. This shrub is readily available in most nurseries and if you incorporate lots of organic matter into the soil and keep it slightly acid, the plants should make vigorous growth and attractive specimens. Plants are reported to be resistant to pollution damage.

Varieties. Picturata (variegated foliage). Dentata (small, coarsely-toothed leaves) 2 feet. Fructu Albo (silver variegated foliage). Goldieana (leaves almost entirely yellow). Longifolia (narrow leaves 5 inches long). Macrophylla (broad, large leaves). Variegata (yellow-spotted leaves). Viridis (green leaves, vigorous variety). 3-4 feet.

Azalea (see Rhododendron, page 46)

Bambusa glaucescens (Multiplex)   **8′ spreads**
Bamboo   **vigorously**
                                        Zone 9

Evergreen member of the grass family, Gramineae.

Characteristics. Bamboo is an invasive, rapidly spreading member of the grass family. It is often used to make an impenetrable hedge.

Bambusa glaucescens (Multiplex).

Culture. Grows vigorously in almost any soil. Best in sun; tolerates shade. Propagated by clump division. For fast screening set clumps 3 feet apart.

Remarks. While bamboo can make a quick screen that gives excellent privacy, its invasiveness can also be a problem. To contain it, use a barrier 24-30 inches into the ground such as old sheets of galvanized roofing or heavy tar paper.

Varieties. Fernleaf (fern-like foliage) and a number of variegated varieties—Alphonse Karr, Silverstripe, and Stripestem Fernleaf.
Chimonobambusa falcata (Bambusa falcata) is a clump-type bamboo, hardy to zone 8 often sold in southern nurseries [4-6 feet].

Berberis Thunbergii   5' x 5'
Japanese Barberry   **Zone 3**

Deciduous or hardy evergreen of the barberry family, Berberidaceae.

Characteristics. Round-headed shrub with slow to moderate growth eventually making a medium-sized plant. Most varieties have thorns that make them relatively impenetrable hedges.

Culture. Tolerant of many soil conditions; good soil preparation with lots of organic matter and good drainage plus attention to watering during dry spells is necessary to keep the plants full and actively growing. Although plants will grow in the shade, the red- or purple-leaved forms will lose their color unless grown in full sun. Several hybrids are available. Prune out old canes in the spring to encourage dense growth. Plant 30 inches apart.

Remarks. This plant is perhaps better adapted to the upper South—zones 7 and 8—but is often used along the Gulf Coast.

Varieties. There are a number of varieties, including one hybrid between B. Thunbergii and B. Julianae, known as B. Mentorensis or Mentor Barberry, which is semi-evergreen to evergreen. It is a large and vigorous shrub [2½ feet]. Other varieties include: Atropurpurea, purple leaves [2 feet]. Aurea, yellow leaves [2 feet]. Erecta, upright branching habit and purple foliage. Compacta [2 feet] Inermis (thornless).

Berberis Julianae, or wintergreen barberry, is another useful evergreen shrub. It grows to 7 feet in height and 3 feet wide and makes a very attractive oval-shaped shrub. It is hardy to zone 6.

Brunfelsia pauciflora   8-12' x 4-6'
Yesterday-Today-and-Tomorrow   **Zone 9**

This is a tender evergreen shrub in the family Solanaceae from South America.

Characteristics. A popular shrub, somewhat tender and deserving a protected location even along the Gulf Coast. It should remain evergreen in tropical areas. It is particularly popular for its flowers, which are very fragrant, phlox-like that open first deep purple then lavender, and finally changing to white. All three colors may appear on the bush at one time. Heavy blooming occurs in the spring. The foliage is an attractive grayish-green.

Culture. Grows in most soils. Will do well in partial shade; along the Gulf Coast it's best in a

Yesterday-today-and tomorrow, flowers (top), foliage and branches (bottom).

protected location such as the south side of a house with tall trees for shade. Plant 30 inches apart.

Remarks. Especially valuable for its intense fragrance and interesting flowers.

Varieties. Several cultivars are listed but are not common in cultivation. Among these are: calycina, with a larger calyx; floribunda, dwarf with abundant flowers [2 feet]; macrantha, large flowers.

Buxus sempervirens   3-6' x 3-6'
Boxwood   **Zone 6**

Evergreen shrub of the family Buxaceae native to Western Europe, Asia, the West Indies, and Central America.

Characteristics. Boxwood's main attribute is that it always appears to be making new growth due to the bright, fresh green appearance of its leaves. Most species are relatively slow-growing and compact. Leaves are oval and small (½ inch in length; ⅜ inch wide).

Culture. Boxwood prefers an acid, organic soil and although it will tolerate heavy soils, iron chlorosis is severe in alkaline soils. Plants will respond to foliar applications of iron chelate but good initial soil preparation is recommended. Boxwood will grow in full sun or partial shade and will withstand frequent shearing. One of the major pests of boxwood is the nematode, a microscopic roundworm which attacks the root system. Since few post-planting nematicides are available now, it is important to consider this potentially disastrous problem before selecting boxwood. Leaf miners can also be a serious problem, disfiguring the plant during early spring. Plant 18-24 inches apart.

Boxwood.

Remarks. Though not showy, boxwood blossoms are rather fragrant.

Varieties. B. microphylla, the Japanese boxwood, as well as many named varieties, including variegated forms of the common boxwood, are also available.

Caesalpinia gilliesii   6-8' x 4'
Bird of Paradise   **Zone 9**

A tender evergreen shrub in the family Leguminosae from South America.

Characteristics. This is a scraggly shrub which is nonetheless spectacular because of its brilliant yellow flowers accented with red stamens. The foliage is fine-textured like that of the mimosa.

Culture. Requires very well-drained soil and full sun in order to be at its best. Don't fertilize or water heavily, especially in late summer or fall, since this plant is tender north of the Gulf Coast. Plant 3 feet apart.

Callicarpa americana   6' x 6'
American Beautyberry,   **Zone 7**
Spanish or French Mulberry

Native to the U.S. in the family Verbenaceae.

Characteristics. Scraggly shrub suitable for use in an informal border or naturalized among trees. Its chief asset is its beautiful violet berries which can be used in flower arrangements.

Culture. Grown in moist soils as an understory planting. Has few insect or disease problems, but is never a very tidy-looking shrub. Plant 3 feet apart.

Remarks. A white-berried form is available and there are a number of other species which would be worthy of trial.

Callistemon citrinus (lanceolatus)   25' x 15'
Lemon Bottlebrush   **Zone 9**
Crimson Bottlebrush

Large shrub of the family Myrtaceae native to Australia.

Flower spikes on bottlebrush.

Characteristics. In areas where temperatures rarely fall below 30°, bottlebrush becomes a rather large plant. However, in lower zone 8 and zone 9 it is severely damaged almost yearly and except for specimens in protected locations, would never attain a 25 foot height. It is valuable for its striking red flowers in spikes to 4 inches long.

Culture. Should be planted on the south side of the house where it will receive full sun. Bottlebrush appreciates good drainage and organic matter mixed with the soil. Avoid watering plants in late summer to harden them off before the first freeze. Plant 6-8 feet apart.

Remarks. This plant attracts hummingbirds. Winter damage often will not show up until early summer, when the demand for water puts the plants under stress and split bark areas from freezing damage take their toll.

Varieties. C. viminalis, or weeping bottlebrush, has bronze-green new foliage and a weeping habit (20 feet x 20 feet). C. rigidus is a narrow, stiff-leaved variety, little used but probably hardier.

Calycanthus floridus   7' x 5'
Carolina Allspice   **Zone 5**
Pineapple Shrub

Deciduous shrub of the family Calycanthaceae.

Characteristics. A shrub featuring dark reddish-brown fragrant flowers in early spring and yellow foliage in the fall.

Culture. Grows best in a rich, well-drained soil with lots of organic matter and an acid pH. Incorporate peat moss and 1-2 lbs. of sulfur per 100

square feet if the soil is known to be alkaline. Plant in sun or partial shade and space 2½ feet apart.

Remarks. Warm, humid weather intensifies flower fragrance.

Varieties. Purpureus with purple leaves. C. fertilis, also called Carolina allspice, is found in Pennsylvania south into Alabama. C. occidentalis is a California native [5 feet].

Camellia japonica   25' x 15'
Camellia   **Zone 8**

Evergreen shrub in the Theaceae family.

Characteristics. The japonicas, though sometimes beautiful as landscape specimens, do have certain drawbacks. The major one is that the flowers, because of their long-lasting nature, hang on the plant well past the time when they are effective and decompose, leaving globs of yucky stuff all over the plants. Under marginal soil conditions, where insufficient organic matter or acidity are a problem, they are generally less vigorous than some of the other species, notably C. sasanqua.

This cluster of bareroot camellias is relatively easy to plant if the tops are pruned back one-half at transplanting to allow for some loss of the root system in the move.

Culture. Camellias require a well-prepared soil in most areas of the South, especially where tight clay or the lack of a rich, loamy soil with an acid pH is available. Planting camellias slightly high, even in ideal soil conditions, is usually advisable and special planting beds may be required (see page 21).

One factor, more than anything else, sets culture of camellias in the South apart from other areas of the country, and that is that the japonica camellias are much easier to grow when grafted on sasanqua rootstock. As you might expect, this is a costly procedure and plants propagated in this manner are more difficult to find and always more expensive. They are, however, infinitely more successful, especially in the southwestern limits of this plant (around Houston, Texas).

Camellias can also be grown in pots, probably the best solution for a clay gumbo soil or limited funds for building beds for shrubs and vines in containers, see page 37). Most standard potting soils can be used if you incorporate sulfur with the mix at the rate of ¼ cup per bushel.

Camellias are generally adapted to shade. Most appreciate a little morning sun, and in good soil some may even tolerate a full day of sun.

The major pest of camellias is teascale. This insect appears as a crusty white substance on the underside of the leaves; the tops of the leaves will usually have a yellow, dappled appearance. These are sucking insects that damage the plant by removing juices. Another symptom is the growth of sooty mold as described under Aucuba. This insect is best controlled with the use of dormant oil spray when temperatures are above 45° and below 85°. A summer dilution of this oil is also effective when temperatures are warmer, but these sprays should be applied in late afternoon or early morning. Test this on a small portion of the plants to determine possible plant damage. Adding an insecticide such as malathion to this summer oil is also effective.

Another serious camellia pest is a fungus disease called dieback (*Glomerella cingulata*). This disease is on the rise in the South and is characterized by dying back of young twigs with eventual death of entire plants. The disease is difficult to control because it enters through wounds either natural or manmade. One of the most critical periods for spray application is when the old leaves begin to shed in early spring. It's also important to treat any pruning cuts. Copper fungicides have been the most effective to date. Petal blight, a serious disease on the West Coast, is thus far of little concern in the South.

Specimens for flower production are often spaced 3 feet apart. Where the plants are allowed to mature, space 8-12 feet apart.

Remarks. The japonica camellias respond readily to applications of gibberellic acid applied in early fall. This growth hormone stimulates earlier flowers that are larger and sometimes variable in color as a result of the treatment. They may also vary in form from this treatment.

There are so many varieties of camellias that it's hard to decide which ones to recommend—books have been written on the subject. In colder areas of the South gardeners should carefully select varieties that flower during the fall or late spring. Mid-season varieties often flower during a period of fluctuating temperatures, resulting in cold injury to blooms or buds. The following selection of varieties from the American Camellia Society's

  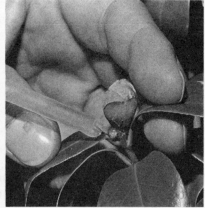

*"Gibbing" japonica camellias. **1**—Flower bud before "gibbing." Smaller bud at the base is a vegetative bud. **2**— Vegetative bud is removed, leaving the small basal cup that supported the bud. **3**—Drops of gibberellic acid applied to the vegetative cup. This treatment supplies the flower bud with an excessive amount of the same growth hormone that produces the normal flower. It will speed up blooming time, increase bloom size, and improve the quality of the flowers.*

Variation in japonica camellia flower forms.

booklet *The Camellia—It's Culture for Beginners* is offered as a starting point:

A Few Suggested Japonica Varieties

Red

Mathotiana
Mathotiana Supreme
Gary's Red
Mark Culver
Forty Niner
John Taylor
Tomorrow
Tom Knudsen
Kramer Supreme

White

Mrs. Hooper Connell
Alba Plena
Charly Bettes
White Empress
Mrs. D.W. Davis
Dear Jenny
Winter Morn
White Nun
Onetia Holland

Pink

Pink Perfection
Guilio Nucoia
Dr. Tinsley
Carters Sunburst
Debutante
Wild Wood
Marie Bracey
Marjorie Magnificent
Rose Parade

Variegated

Extravaganza
Same Var.
Ville DeNantes
Lady Kay
Rosea Superba
Mathotiana Var.
Carter Sunburst
Pink Var.
Tiffany
Commander Mulroy

Camellia Sasanqua   **15' x 15'**
Sasanqua Camellia   **Zone 8**

Evergreen shrub of the Theaceae family.

Characteristics. This plant is of particular value for use in the shade where an attractive, vigorous, dense shrub with winter flower color is desired. It is slightly less finicky in its cultural requirements than the japonica camellia, and although it suffers from similar pests, most gardeners consider it a much easier shrub to grow. Camellia fanciers often look down on the sasanqua because its blossoms do not hold well when cut. As discussed under the japonica types though, this is a landscape advantage since the petals rapidly shatter, fall to the ground, and decompose.

Culture. Sasanquas are usually listed as being hardier than the japonicas, but the opposite is suggested by the National Arboretum in Washington, D.C., based on their observations in the gardens there. Where winter hardiness is not a concern, the above-mentioned increased vigor is a major attribute. They respond to the same soil requirements and pest control suggestions listed for japonicas. Space 6-8 feet apart.

Sasanqua camellia.

Some of the More Vigorous Sasanqua Camellias

Variety	Sasanqua Form	Color
Apple Blossom	single	white, pink blush
Australian Hiryu	semi-double	rose-red
Bonanza	semi-peony	red
Chansonette	formal double	pink
Cleopatra	semi-double	pink
Dawn	semi-double	white, pink blush
Hana Jiman	single	white, pink tip
Hugh Evans	single	pink
Jean May	double	pink
Ko-Gyoku	formal double	white, edged pink
Little Pearl	semi-double	white, pink buds
Narumigata	single	white, pink blush
Pink Snow	anemone	light pink
Rainbow	single	white, red border
Setsugekka	semi-double	white, ruffled petals
Shinonome	single to semi-double	pink
Shishi-Gashira	double	red
Showa-No-Sakae	semi-double	pink
Sparkling Burgundy	peony	dark pink
White Cleopatra	semi-double	white
White Doves	semi-double	white
Yal Arare	single	white, edged pink
Yuletide	single	orange and red
Camellia rosiflora	single, small	pink

Some of the More Vigorous Camellia Hybrids

Variety	Form	Color
Baby Face	rose	pink
Betty Ridley	formal double	pink
Coral Delight	semi-double	coral pink
Dr. Clifford Parks	anemone	red
El Dorado	peony	light pink
Fragrant Pink	loose peony	pink
Francie L.	semi-double	pink
Freedom Bell	semi-double	red
Glenn's Orbit	loose peony	orchid-pink
Harold Paige	double	red
K.O. Hester	semi-double	pink
Lasca Beauty	semi-double	pink
Lilette Witman	loose peony	pink, silvery blush
Miss Tulare	peony	rose-red
Nuccios's Rudy	semi-double, ruffled	red
Ole	rose	pink
Peking	semi-double	pink
Royalty	semi-double	pink to red
South Seas	semi-double	silver pink
Terrell Weaver	semi-double	red
Tiptoe	semi-double	pink
Valley Knudsen	semi-double	orchid-pink
Wilber Foss	peony	pinkish-red

Varieties. The following table is a guide to some of the finest sasanquas. But for the collector, several other Camellia species are worth growing. One, C. hiemalis, is often listed separately but is suggested in *Hortus Third* as only a form of C. sasanqua. C. reticulata is a large shrub with huge flowers but lacking vigor and thus it is difficult to grow. Hybrids of reticulata with japonica and several other species have proved to be worthy of culture.

Varieties and/or hybrids of C. salicifolia and C. saluenensis have also been valuable. The common Tea plant, C. sinensis, makes an interesting hedge and has attractive single flowers with many prominent yellow stamens. It would be very easy to grow all the tea you needed with just a few bushes. It is reported that some varieties of the sasanqua camellia are also used for tea.

Carissa grandiflora	**4-6′ x 4-6′**
Natal Plum	**Lower Zone 9**

Evergreen shrubs primarily from tropical Africa but also found from India to Indonesia. Dogbane family (Apocynaceae).

Characteristics. Glossy, green foliage, fragrant flowers, and tart, red, plum-like fruits are the main attractions of this shrub. Most varieties have spiny growth and thus are somewhat childproof.

Natal plum. These fragrant flowers are followed by tart, plum-like fruits.

Culture. The natal plum is of major importance along the lower Gulf Coast because, although it is rather tender, it is quite salt tolerant. Good drainage and full sun are a must; plants may be grown further inland in protected locations. Standard varieties should be planted 24-30 inches apart; however, many dwarf forms have been developed, so closer spacing is often used.

Remarks. The natal plum should only be used in protected locations in zone 9 because of its sensitivity to cold damage.

Varieties. Fancy, with large-sized fruit. Green Carpet, low-growing, spreading habit with fine-textured foliage. Prostrate natal plum, vigorous spreading habit for use as a groundcover. Ruby-point, with red tips. Tomlinson, semi-thornless dwarf. Tuttlei, compact and early-bearing.

Cassia corymbosa   **10' x 5'**
Flowery senna   **Zone 9**

An evergreen large shrub of the family Leguminosae (subfamily Caesalpinioideae).

Characteristics. A very tough upright shrub that is fast-growing with bright yellow blooms in mid-summer.

Culture. This plant needs little more than to be put into the ground. It makes a beautiful accent shrub which can be espaliered against a wall. Plant 3-5 feet apart. Protect somewhat in winter, especially in the regions further from the coast.

Varieties. Cassia mexicana, which is usually a shrub but can be grown as a small tree, is hardy to zone 8. Although not readily available, it should be

Flowery senna.

tried in southern nurseries. C. splendida blooms in the fall (November) and looks very much like C. corymbosa (showier and larger leaflets) but is reliably hardy only in zone 10 and warmer climates. It will recover from the rootstock when frozen to the ground in zone 8.

Cestrum nocturnum   **8-12' x 8'**
Night-Scented Jasmine   **Zone 9**

An evergreen shrub of the Solanaceae family.

Characteristics. An extremely fragrant (at night) shrub with narrow shiny leaves and greenish-white flowers up to 1 inch long but not especially showy.

Culture. Grows well in most soils but appreciates the addition of 2-4 inches of organic matter such as peat moss or finely ground pine bark. Often freezes to the ground in zone 8—needs a protected location there. Plant 3 feet apart.

Remarks. Delightful to plant under a bedroom window or near an outside living area for its evening fragrance.

Varieties. Reportedly, in South Africa, there are a number of forms including ones with flowers in pink and dark purple shades.

Chaenomeles speciosa   **3-4' x 3-4'**
Flowering Quince   **Zone 5**

Deciduous or semi-evergreen woody shrubs of the Rosaceae family including three to four species native to Eastern Asia and many hybrids.

Characteristics. The main attribute of the flowering quince is that it is one of the earliest to bloom of all shrubs. In the lower South it is semi-evergreen. Its flowers are not nearly as showy as some other shrubs because the blossoms are borne on the interior of the plant. Fruit, if it sets, does have a nice fragrance. Cut stems are also valuable for forcing the blossoms indoors during the winter. Plant 30 inches apart.

Culture. There are no particular requirements for this shrub. It is very easy to grow and can be grown in partial shade as well as full sun. Being a member of the rose family, some varieties may be rather susceptible to fire blight, a bacterial dis-

Summer-sweet.

Flowering quince, one of the earliest-blooming of all shrubs.

ease. Spraying with a copper fungicide during blooming should reduce infection, but the blue color of the copper fungicide would destroy the main feature of this plant—its delicate blossoms. Plant 2-3 feet apart.

Varieties. The list of varieties could be almost endless for this genus, but there seems to be an increasing tendency on the part of the southern nurserymen not to list varieties at all but simply to depend on the plant's selling in early spring because they'll bloom before most other plants.

Some of the more common varieties: Fire Chief, red. Ruby Glow, pinkish red. Alba, white. A number of varieties may be hybrids between the Japanese Quince (C. speciosa) and the lesser flowering quince, C. japonica. These hybrids are sometimes designated C. x superba.

Clethra alnifolia   10' x 6'
Summer-sweet (Sweet Pepperbush)   **Zone 5**

Deciduous shrub of the Clethraceae family.

Characteristics. A large semi-evergreen shrub which blooms with tiny bell-like blossoms in July. Flowers fragrant.

Culture. Grows best in a sandy, wet soil, and although it ranges from New England to Texas, it is rarely used in the South. Plants grown from the southern seed source could be much more commonly used in southern landscapes. Plant 3 feet apart.

Varieties. C. alnifolia rosea, a form with pinkish flowers, has been reported. C. pringlei is an evergreen tree (to 4 feet in zone 8) native to northeastern Mexico. It is hardy to the lower region of zone 8 but is not available in the nursery trade.

Cocculus laurifolius   15' x 12'
Snail Seed   **Zone 9**

Lustrous evergreen shrub of the family Menispermaceae.

Characteristics. This is a plant that always looks as if it has just been shined. It has a coarse texture and although an upright shrub, the branches fall gracefully in a pendulous manner. Leaf veins are prominent and the shiny leaves have a leathery texture.

Culture. Well adapted to the shade, prefers a rich organic soil that is well drained. Cocculus is not drought-tolerant. Plant 6 feet apart.

Remarks. A valuable native vine in the same genus is also available: C. carolinus, Carolina Moonseed. It has shiny leaves and attractive red berries.

Cortaderia selloana   10' x 6'
Pampas Grass   **Zone 7**

Shrub-like grass native to Argentina in the family Graminaceae.

Though not technically a shrub, this plant is often used in place of one, and because of its dense, fast-growing nature, it makes an excellent screen spaced about 4-6 feet apart. It should be planted in full sun. Pampas grass reportedly attracts snakes to the dense cover. Plants are frequently sheared back in the spring to promote new growth. In summer and fall they produce beautiful plume-like flower heads. A pink variety is reported but is not nearly as showy as the white-flowered form.

Cotoneaster species   3' x 4'
Cotoneaster   **Zone 5**

Evergreen shrubs in the family Rosaceae.

Characteristics. Many of the cotoneasters are used for groundcovers, but there are shrubby forms that are typically slow-growing, at least where they are best-adapted—in dry, arid climates. They produce fruit varying from red to orange.

Culture. The major difficulty with cotoneasters is that most are rather susceptible to fire blight, a bacterial disease. If cotoneasters are to be used, it may be necessary to spray them during the blooming period with a copper fungicide to reduce fire blight infection. Otherwise, full sun and good drainage are important. Most have good salt tolerance and may have value for seashore planting. They are reportedly deer-resistant. Space 2 feet apart.

Varieties. C. glaucophyllus is an evergreen shrub 4-6 feet in height with arching growth habit. Hardy to zone 7, it produces white flowers and orange fruit ¼ inch in diameter. A native of China.

C. horizontalis is often sold in the nursery trade for groundcover use. It needs full sun, good drainage and is rather susceptible to fire blight.

C. lacteus (Parneyi) is an evergreen shrub 10-12 feet tall with an arching growth habit. It is hardy to zone 7 and native to western China. White flowers are followed by red fruit ¼ inch in length.

C. pannosus, an evergreen shrub hardy to zone 7, is native to China. It has dull green leaves and white flowers followed by red fruit ¼ inch in diameter. This species also has a dwarf variety, 'Nanus.'

Duranta repens   6-15' x 6-15'
Golden-dewdrop (Skyflower)   **Zone 9**

A tender, evergreen shrub in the family Verbenaceae native to southern Florida, Central and South America.

Characteristics. This is an old-fashioned shrub not seen much in nurseries, perhaps because of the extremely poisonous yellow berries that it produces. It is valuable, however, for the profuse lilac flowers produced at the ends of branches during the summer.

Culture. Very easy to grow in almost any soil. Best planted in a protected location since it often freezes

back in its northern range. Easily grown from seed or cuttings. Plant 3-5 feet apart.

Varieties. Alba, white flowers. Grandiflora, larger flowers. Variegata, variegated foliage. Since even the standard variety is no longer common, these may not be available except in rare plant collections.

Elaeagnus pungens   8-15' x 8'
Thorny Elaeagnus (Silver Berry)   **Zone 7**

Evergreen woody shrub from China and Japan in the family Elaeagnaceae.

Characteristics. A dense mounded shrub with an overall silvery gray appearance. It is a beautiful shrub valued mainly for its attractive silvery foliage but the obscure flowers are also quite fragrant in the fall, hence the species name, *pungens*.

Culture. Easy to grow and tolerant of most soils, but like most plants, it appreciates the addition of organic matter and yearly fertilization. The major pest of Elaeagnus is the spider mite. It can be controlled with three kelthane applications at weekly intervals. In areas heavily wooded with pines, the pine mouse can be a serious pest. The rodents chew the roots and girdle the plant at the soil surface or slightly below. Plant 3 feet apart.

Remarks. The fruit of this shrub is edible when ripe and can be used to make jellies. Another species, E. multiflora, the Cherry Elaeagnus or Gumi, is a 6-foot deciduous shrub which produces its flowers in the spring. The fruit is a very attractive metallic red color and makes excellent jelly. In addition, this latter species is hardy to zone 5.

Varieties. A number of varieties of thorny elaeagnus have been named including Aurea with yellow-margined leaves and Compacta which is a dwarf [24 inches].

Euonymus americana   8' x 4'
Strawberry Bush   **Zone 5**

Semi-evergreen shrub native from New York and south to Florida and Texas. Many species in the family are native to Asia, Europe, Africa, and Australia. Family Celastraceae.

Strawberry bush—closeup of the seed. Oval-shaped structures at bottom are arils, or fleshy seed coverings, that are a brilliant red color.

Japanese aralia.

Characteristics. This is certainly one of the more obscure Euonymus species in the nursery trade and perhaps we're including it out of spite for all the gaudy goldspot euonymus (E. japonica) that have been sold. The main feature of the strawberry bush is its seed with a bright red aril, or fleshy seed covering.

Culture. This particular species will especially appreciate a sandy, acid soil with lots of organic matter incorporated. It does best in partial shade. Many other species will grow if almost thrown out on the ground. Plant 2-2½ feet apart.

Remarks. The main objection to some of the more common varieties of euonymus, especially E. japonica, is that they're susceptible to a great many insect and disease problems, notably scale insects like the euonymus scale or Florida wax scale and powdery mildew. Though these pests can be controlled, it's a difficult, uphill fight once they get a firm hold on the plant. Another shrubby euonymus species that might be tried is the winged euonymus, E. alata.

Fatsia japonica (Aralia japonica)   6-8' x 8'
Paper Plant or Japanese Aralia   **Zone 8**
(Japanese Fatsia)

A coarse-textured evergreen shrub of the family Araliaceae.

Characteristics. A very tropical-looking shrub for a shaded location. Very tough and easy to grow. May sun-scald if given West sun.

Culture. Needs to be planted in a shaded or partially shaded area with a rich organic soil. Some winter damage may occur but the plant quickly grows out of it in the spring. Plant 3-4 feet apart.

Varieties. A compact growth form, Moseri, and a variegated form are listed.

Feijoa sellowiana   18' x 10'
Pineapple Guava   **Lower Zone 8**

Evergreen shrub native to South America and a member of the family Myrtaceae.

Characteristics. A very tough, hardy shrub or small tree with grayish-green foliage. It produces

Pineapple guava. The stamens of this flower are bright red; the petals are edible and quite tasty.

beautiful single flowers with bright red stamens and fleshy petals that are rather tasty in salads. The fruit can also be used to make a good jelly which has a guava-like flavor. This is one of the most attractive shrubs that can be used as a small multi-trunked tree. It is long-lived, though somewhat slow-growing. If the tree form is desired, the wait is worthwhile.

Culture. Easy to grow, it prefers to be in full sun and is sometimes attacked by scale insects which can be controlled with a dormant oil during the winter or with sprays of malathion during the summer. Plant 4-5 feet apart.

Varieties. A number of varieties are listed but are rarely offered in nurseries.

Gardenia jasminoides   6′ x 6′
Gardenia (Cape Jasmine)   **Zone 8**

Tender evergreen shrub in the family Rubiaceae. Most are native to tropical Africa.

Characteristics. Beautiful evergreen foliage and richly aromatic white flowers. The most popular varieties are double or semi-double but there are also some interesting single-flower forms.

Culture. Gardenias appreciate an acid soil with lots of organic matter and grow best in partial shade or where they get morning sun and afternoon shade. They are extremely susceptible to whitefly damage and this will be a constant battle. Using dormant oils or summer oil plus malathion or cygon sprays can effectively control this pest. They are also susceptible to nematode damage and if a plant dies from nematodes, it may be necessary to sterilize the soil prior to replanting in the same area. Plant 3 feet apart.

Gardenia flowers are extremely fragrant. The foliage is evergreen and lustrous.

Remarks. Although many species (approximately 200) exist, most of the forms in the nurseries trade are actually jasminoides. The dwarf gardenia is one good example. It has smaller leaves and small flowers but is often listed as a separate species, G. radicans (2 feet).

Hibiscus syriacus   6-10′ x 4-6′
Rose-of-Sharon, Althaea   **Zone 5**

A deciduous shrub native to Asia in the family Malvaceae.

Characteristics. A rather upright-growing shrub or small multi-trunk tree primarily valuable for its attractive single or double flowers varying in color from white to blue to pink.

Rose-of-Sharon.

Culture. Easily grown in almost any soil; prefers full sun. It is often attacked by aphids in the early spring. Sprays of malathion or nicotine sulphate will easily control this pest. Plant 4 feet apart.

Varieties. Admiral Dewey, with double white flowers. Lucy, semi-double rose-colored flowers. Blue Bird, single blue flowers with a dark center.

Hydrangea quercifolia   6-10′ x 5-8′
Oakleaf Hydrangea   **Zone 5**

Deciduous shrub native to the southeastern United States in the family Saxifragaceae.

Characteristics. This is a striking plant in bloom and it is equally valued for its large, oak-like

Flowers and foliage of the oakleaf hydrangea.

leaves. The clusters of small white flowers are much like regular hydrangeas, but the clusters are more elongated. This particular species requires an acid, well-drained soil in order to grow well, whereas the more common H. macrophylla will grow in most soils provided it's given enough water.

Culture. Water is the key to success with hydrangeas, but good drainage and plenty of organic matter are also important. They need to be planted in partial shade to do their best but will grow rather well with morning sun. Prune after flowering. Space 3 feet apart.

Remarks. The common hydrangea, H. macrophylla (2½ feet), is capable of producing different flower colors depending on the pH of the soil. If the soil is acid, the flowers are blue; if the soil is alkaline, they're pink. Acidity can be provided with aluminum sulphate or with incorporation of sulfur in the soil prior to planting at the rate of 2 pounds

per 100 square feet. Alkalinity can be provided by using lime at 5 pounds per 100 square feet. Not all varieties will respond this way but the most common ones will. H. macrophylla needs an east exposure and lots of water.

Varieties. Two varieties—Harmony with double, sterile flowers and Snow Flake, another double flowered variety—are available and do well in the South.

Ilex cassine 15-40′ x 8-15′
Dahoon Holly **Zone 7**

Evergreen shrub or small tree in the holly family, Aquifoliaceae native to the southeastern United States.

Characteristics. This evergreen tree with narrow lanceolate leaves is much neglected in southern landscapes. As with most hollies, there are male and female plants. The females are desired because of their berry production. Nevertheless, some male plants are necessary. Cross pollination with other species such as male Yaupon Hollies may suffice to produce berries.

Culture. Most hollies are easy to grow although they vary in their demands for acid soil and their subsequent susceptibility to iron chlorosis. The Dahoon Holly has a particularly high demand for iron and thus an acid soil high in organic matter is recommended. If iron chlorosis shows up, sprays of iron chelate may be necessary. Leaf miners, the

Dahoon holly, a shrub or small tree that grows to 30 feet tall.

larvae of small insects, tunnel between the cell layers and may sometimes be a problem. Dimethoate, a systemic foliar insecticide, can be used for treatment of this pest as well as for scale insects which may also cause trouble. Space 6 feet apart.

Remarks. A tea is sometimes prepared from the dried or roasted leaves of this plant.

Varieties. Dodd's and Willow Leaf. Lowei, yellow-fruited form.

Ilex cornuta	**8-10' x 4-8'**
Chinese Holly	**Zone 7**

Evergreen shrub in the holly family.

Characteristics. This is a beautiful glossy green-leaved holly which is very commonly used in southern landscapes. One of its common names, Horned Holly, is a fitting description, for the common species has very prominent spines along the leaf margins. An equally common variety, Burford Holly, has only one spine, at the apex of the leaf. Whereas most holly species require a male for pollination, the Chinese Holly will usually set seed without a male pollinator.

Culture. Grows in most soils with little care; however, it does have several serious diseases, most notably tea scale, an insect which also attacks camellia plants. Where this pest is found, insecticides as described for I. cassine can be used. A dormant oil can be used when temperatures are below 45° for at least a 48-hour period. Plant 2-3 feet apart.

Varieties. There are a great many varieties. The most notable one is Burford described above. There are also compact forms (2 feet) of both the Burford and regular Chinese Holly, often denoted Rotunda, although there is an Ilex rotunda which is an entirely different species.

Ilex crenata	**4' x 2½'**
Japanese Holly	**Zone 6**

Evergreen shrub small in the holly family.

Characteristics. This small holly is frequently seen as a dwarf hedge. Its leaves are typically glossy and are reminiscent of those of boxwood. The plant produces black berries that are not very prominent.

Culture. Same as for other hollies. Prefers a slightly acid soil. Scale insects can occasionally be a pest.

Varieties. Many varieties are offered, and most differ in shape and texture of leaves.

Ilex decidua	**15-30' x 8-15'**
Possum Haw (Deciduous Holly)	**Zone 5**

Deciduous shrub or small multi-trunk tree in the holly family.

Characteristics. This is another neglected native holly. It looks much like the yaupon during the summer when it has foliage. It loses its foliage in

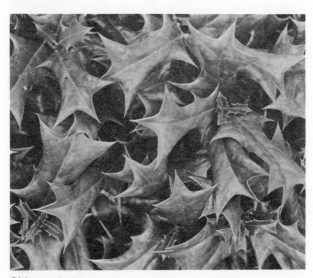

Chinese holly.

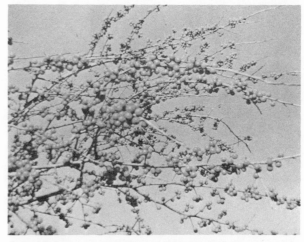

Possum haw, or deciduous holly. It's easy to see where the plant gets its name from. After losing its foliage, the female plant bears bright red berries.

the winter, and the female plants carry bright red berries throughout that season. They last so long, in fact, that by spring they still remain and have bleached to an orange color.

Culture. Same for other hollies. Plant 8 feet apart.

Remarks. Since this species does require cross pollination from male plants, some nurseries have grafted one male branch on the female plants thus guaranteeing fruit set.

Varieties. A number of varieties have been offered, primarily by Warrens Nursery in Oklahoma City. These include a yellow-berried variety, Byer's Golden, Oklahoma, and Warren's Red.

Ilex vomitoria	**20′ x 10′**
Yaupon	**Zone 7**

Evergreen shrub or small multi-trunk in the holly family.

Characteristics. Perhaps the most adaptable of all southern hollies, it will grow in acid soils as well as neutral to slightly alkaline soils. It is very popular in its dwarf form.

Culture. Leaf miners in the early spring are one of the major problems and can be controlled as described under I. cassine. Plant 5 feet apart.

Remarks. This shrub is also used sometimes to make a bitter tea from the dried or roasted leaves.

Varieties. Many varieties have been introduced including weeping forms and the dwarf forms. (1½-2 feet) The latter are especially popular for use in foundation plannings in southern landscapes.

Dwarf yaupon. This popular shrub does well in pots and is a good candidate for topiary (see page 11). Untrained, it makes an attractive low hedge.

Other Hollies

Ilex aquifolium. English Holly is little used in the lower South and is more of a tree than a shrub (8 feet). Ilex fosteri, a hybrid variety with narrow leaflets and a heavy set of red berries. Juvenile form pyramidal. (4 feet).

Ilex glabra. Inkberry (Gallberry) and I. coriacea are native to the South but are rarely used. Both have black berries (4-6 feet).

Ilex opaca. The American holly is more of a tree than a shrub, but it may be trained to the latter form. There are many cultivars; most have spiny leaves and red berries. (10-15 feet).

Ilex rotunda. This is an oriental species with smooth leaf margins. It is more tree-like but may be used as a large, evergreen hedge plant. Females have red berries. (8-12 feet).

Illicium floridanum	**10′ x 8′**
Star Purple Anise (Florida Anise)	**Zone 8**

An evergreen shrub in the family Illiciaceae.

Characteristics. A valuable evergreen shrub because of its beautiful coarse-textured, glossy leaves and its attractive purplish-red flowers which, unfortunately, are not very prominent because they tend to be pointed downward or hidden by the foliage.

Culture. This plant requires a sandy acid soil rich in organic matter. Plant 4-5 feet apart. White flies can be a serious pest.

Star purple anise.

Varieties. Another species, I. anisatum, the Japanese Anise Tree, is larger and more vigorous, reaching 15-20 feet with fragrant yellowish-green flowers that are not as showy. Because the plant will tolerate more sun and heavier soils, it deserves more use. Anise would make a fascinating subject for a southern plant breeding project.

Itea virginica	10' x 6'
Sweetspire	**Zone 6**

Deciduous shrub in the family Saxifragaceae native to the southeastern United States.

Characteristics. Fragrant white flowers in racemes 4-6 inches long and brilliant red fall color are the main attributes of this plant.

Sweetspire bearing racemes of its fragrant white flowers.

Culture. They will grow in most soils and are tolerant of shade as well as sun. Very tolerant of excess moisture. Plant 3 feet apart.

Remarks. Not common in nurseries. Deserves more use.

Jasminum humile	10-20' x 5-10'
Italian Jasmine	**Zone 8**

Evergreen shrub native to western China in the Jasmine family Oleaceae.

Characteristics. This is a vigorous upright-growing shrub covered with beautiful yellow flowers in late spring.

Culture. Easily grown in most soils. Blooms best in full sun. Plant 3-4 feet apart.

Varieties. J. floridum is a similar plant, lower-growing and semi-evergreen, which blooms later in the summer.

Jasminum mesnyi	6-10' x 6-8'
Primrose Jasmine	**Zone 8**

Evergreen shrub native to China, family Oleaceae.

Characteristics. The fountain-like growth habit of this plant makes it especially valuable for a cascading effect. Its extremely early spring flowers are an additional reward. It is a very tough shrub, drought-tolerant, and relatively free of insect and disease damage.

Flower of primrose jasmine. This shrub blooms early in spring.

Culture. Easy to grow in most soils. Needs full sun for good blooming. Plant 6 feet apart.

Varieties. J. nudiflorum has a similar growth habit but is deciduous and is hardier to zone 6.

Lagerstroemia indica	4-8' x 4-6'
Dwarf Crapemyrtle	**Zone 7**

Deciduous shrub in the family Lythraceae native to Asia.

Characteristics. These plants are essentially miniature crapemyrtles and are especially valuable because they don't quickly grow into trees under southern growing conditions. (Actually, some varieties do grow quite tall: Fire Bird up to 20 feet; New Snow, to 12 feet; and Weeping Pink are examples.) Eventually, however, they would make very interesting multi-trunk specimen trees if trained properly. A number of cultivars are available with flower colors from white through pinks, reds, and purples.

Dwarf crapemyrtle trained as a multitrunked tree (top) and as a specimen in a large tub (bottom).

Culture. To date, most of the Dwarf Crapemyrtles seem to have at least a normal susceptibility to powdery mildew. Some may be more susceptible than the larger cultivars. They are also attacked by scale insects and crapemyrtle aphid. Benomyl, a systemic fungicide, is good for prevention of mildew if sprayed in early spring when the leaves are approximately half mature and then again when fully matured. Crapemyrtles need full sun and good air circulation. This alone will reduce mildew infection. Pruning the plant back to ground level in late winter aids in maintaining a dense low plant with excellent flowers. Plant 3 feet apart.

Varieties. Pink Ruffle, with rosy-pink flowers. Tiny Fire, with reddish pink flowers. Snow White, white flowers with fringed petals.

Laurus nobilis	10-40' x 6-15'
True Laurel (Bay Laurel)	**Zone 9**

Evergreen shrub or small tree native to the Mediterranean. A member of the family Lauraceae.

Characteristics. Often grown as a sheared hedge, it makes a very dense impenetrable plant when used this way. Its bright, shiny green leaves are its most notable attraction, and they're also the bay leaves used in cooking.

Culture. The true laurel appreciates a well-drained acid soil that's been enriched with peat moss. Unfortunately, it has limited use because of its lack of cold hardiness, but it's highly recommended where it can be grown. Plant 4 feet apart.

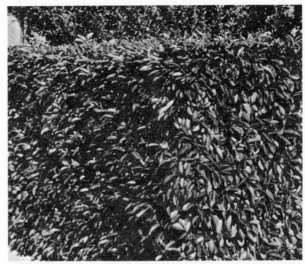

A hedge of true laurel. The foliage, outstanding in its own right, is the bay leaf used in cooking.

Varieties. A number of varieties have been listed, including the willow-leaf bay, L. angustifolia, L. aurea (yellow leaves), L. undulata with wavy leaf margins.

Leucophyllum frutescens   4-8′ x 4-6′
Texas Purple Sage (Ceniza)   **Zone 8**

Gray-leaved evergreen shrub native to Texas and Mexico in the family Scrophulariaceae.

Characteristics. This plant is especially valuable for its grayish green foliage and the beautiful lilac to purple-colored flowers that appear following a rain.

Culture. Texas Purple Sage demands full sun, good drainage and a neutral to slightly alkaline soil. Thus in some areas it may be necessary to mix 5 pounds of lime per 100 square feet before planting. If the soil is a tight clay, planting in raised beds is advisable.
   This is one plant that seems to thrive especially well when planted in service station islands, no doubt because of the neglect and the heat from surrounding concrete. If given too much care in the form of water and fertilizer, it becomes tall and scraggly. Plant 2½ feet apart.
   A minimum of pruning may be necessary to keep the plant looking shapely, and this is best done after the first spring bloom.

Varieties. A number of colorful variants, from white to dark purple have been found.

Leucothoe populifolia   8-12′ x 4-6′
Florida Leucothoe   **Zone 7**

Evergreen shrub native to the United States in the family Ericaceae.

Characteristics. Beautiful waxy green foliage is this plant's main attribute. It is not a plant that lends itself to trimming and is more at home in a loose open border situation. The new growth is often vigorous and gives the plant a somewhat scraggly appearance. It is, nevertheless, an excellent plant for the shade.

Culture. A sandy, acid soil and full or partial shade are necessary for this plant to do well. Plant 2½-3 feet apart.

Florida leucothoe.

Varieties. Several other species including Asian species, are worth trying in the southern landscape. L. Fontanesiana, (often sold as L. Catesbaei), commonly known as drooping leucothoe, is another native species hardy to zone 5 which is sometimes offered in the nursery trade. It is less vigorous than L. populifolia. Another interesting leucothoe is L. axillaris, with very fragrant flowers.

Ligustrum japonicum   10-15′ x 8-10′
Wax-leaf Ligustrum   **Zone 7**

Evergreen shrub native to Japan and Korea in the family Oleaceae.

Characteristics. This is one of the most common of all landscape plants in the South. It makes a dense, beautiful, glossy green hedge and can be sheared at will or left to grow in its natural form. It has a lighter green foliage color and is more shrub-like than a similar species, Ligustrum lucidum, discussed below.

Culture. This plant will grow in almost any soil, but like most shrubs it will respond to adequate fertilization and incorporation of 2-4 inches of organic matter in the soil prior to planting. It is easily propagated from 8- to 12-inch cuttings made in June. Plant 3-4 feet apart.

Wax-leaf ligustrum.

Glossy privet grown as a multitrunk tree.

As with any plant, if enough are used, insects or diseases will find them sooner or later. This seems to be the case with the waxleaf ligustrum. Fungal leaf spot often partially defoliates the shrubs during the summer, so sprays of a fungicide to prevent this defoliation may be necessary. Spraying prior to the occurrence of this disease is the key, and these sprays will be needed in May, June, and July. Whiteflies are also a pest with ligustrum; they can be controlled as discussed under Gardenias, page 29.

Varieties. A variegated variety is listed. L. texanum is a species often listed in nursery catalogs as being more dense-growing. Another species, L. coriaceum (curly-leaf ligustrum), is curious, although somewhat grotesque. Its leaves have notches at the tips, and they tend to curl, giving L. coriaceum a motley appearance.

Ligustrum lucidum   30′ x 10-15′
Glossy Privet   **Zone 8**

Evergreen shrub or small tree native to China and Korea in the family Oleaceae.

Characteristics. This plant has a darker green leaf, not quite as glossy as the wax-leaf ligustrum, and is often more upright, making a large hedge or small tree.

Culture. Whiteflies are also a problem on this shrub. Control as for gardenias. Plant 8-10 feet apart. Growing requirements are similar to L. japonicum.

Remarks. The glossy privet often sets huge quantities of purple berries that are terribly messy and not very ornamental.

Varieties. A great many varieties of L. lucidum are offered, primarily those with yellow variegation. There are also many other species of Ligustrum in the nursery trade, though wax-leaf ligustrum and glossy privet are the two most commonly used in southern landscapes. L. vulgare, the Common Privet (2 feet), is often advertised for mail order and may occasionally end up in southern gardens. It is hardy to zone 5, and in upper regions of the South (zones 6 and 7) it has some utility, but even there it is rather weedy, and it is deciduous.

Lindera benzoin   6-15′ x 5-10′
Spicebush   **Zone 4**

A deciduous shrub native to North America in the family Lauraceae.

Characteristics. This shrub has a rather open growth habit. It has coarse-textured, light green foliage that is very aromatic with a distinct lemon fragrance. Foliage turns yellow in the fall.

Culture. Spicebush grows best in a loose, sandy soil. However, because of its tremendous range from southern Maine to Texas, there is considerable variation in the requirements of plants depending on the origin of seed. In some areas, especially drier areas of the South such as central Texas, it is a rather rare plant. Plant 4 feet apart.

Varieties. Other species, such as L. melissifolia (Jove's fruit), a deciduous shrub found in wet locations in the Southeast, L. obtusiloba, and Asian species to 20 feet tall, and L. umbellata, also an Asian species, deserve more trial in southern landscapes.

Shrubs for Patios and Containers

Container gardening is extremely popular for a number of reasons. To begin with, it allows gardeners who don't have a landscape an opportunity to grow many of their favorite plants, and it makes these plants very portable so they can be moved inside for protection from winter cold or to the patio if a party is planned. And if the plants look bad, they can be shifted to a recovery site until they're more presentable.

Usually we think of planting annual flowers like petunias and marigolds in containers, but many shrubs are also well adapted to container gardening, and they have the distinct advantage of being more permanent and easier to care for.

Almost any container can be used for shrubs, but large wooden tubs or pots at least 10 inches in diameter are usually necessary. The soil mix is especially important when planting shrubs. It should be a fast-draining soil mix, and definitely not soil dug out of the backyard. Some of the synthetic soil mixes (which contain no soil) are especially useful. But they drain *so* well that frequent watering is necessary—once or even twice a day in summer. Experimentation, to strike some happy medium which will reduce watering and yet provide excellent drainage, is recommended.

Shrubs from arid climates obviously will need a looser mix and less water than shrubs adapted to wet soil conditions (see the lists on pages 3-4). Adequate drainage holes in the container are necessary if the plants are going to live for any length of time.

When planting shrubs in containers, be sure you loosen the root system, even going to the extreme of cutting it lengthwise along the surface of the root ball to spread the roots out into the surrounding potting soil. Otherwise, the plants will remain root-bound and limp along for awhile, eventually dying. Since this removal of roots is going to make the plant less able to support the top of the plant, removing one-third to one-half of the top is also recommended.

Regular fertilization will also be required. You can use one of the soluble houseplant fertilizers, half-strength every 2 weeks during the growing season, or better yet, one of the slow-release pellet-type fertilizers that meter out a little bit of nutrient solution every time you water.

Some of the shrubs best adapted to container growing include true bay, (Laurus nobilis), genetic dwarf nectarines such as Silver Prolific and Southern Belle; dwarf peaches like Empress, Southern Rose and Southern Sweet; variegated pittosporum or Wheelers' pittosporum (dwarf, plain green variety); gold dust plant (aucuba); azalea; yesterday-today-tomorrow plant (Brunfelsia); boxwood (Buxus); bougainvillea; Japanese camellias, Sasanqua camellias; flowering quince (Chaenomeles); silverberry (Elaeagnus); fatshedera (vine-like fatsia); gardenia; dwarf holly (Ilex); Mahonia fortunei (shade); Mahonia lomariifolia (shade to partial shade); nandina; dwarf oleander (Nerium); Philodendron selloum; Japanese black pine (Pinus thunbergii); lady palm (Rhapis excelsa, for shade); Cleyera (Ternstroemia); miniature roses; and abelia.

Potting Soil Mixes

The soil mixes given below are for filling planter boxes, for container gardening, or for gardening in areas behind retaining walls on rocky hillsides where there is little or no soil. The mixes are designed for season-long use without feeding. Amounts are by volume.

Procedure: mix, moisten, set in a warm place, and allow to incubate a month before planting.

Mix #1	*Mix #3*
2 parts sand or loam (66%)	4 parts sand or loam (44%)
1 part manure (33%)	4 parts S.A.* (44%)
¼ cup 0-20-0	1 part compost (12%)
Mix #2	*Mix #4*
3 parts sand or loam (43%)	4 parts sand or loam (40%)
3 parts S.A.* (43%)	5 parts S.A.* (30%)
1 part manure or cottonseed meal (14%)	1 part clay (10%) 2 parts manure (20%)

Note: Before adding manure to mixes, add 2 oz. super-phosphate (0-20-0) per gallon of manure. If soil pH is under 6.0, add 1 level tablespoonful of limestone per gallon of mix.

*Soil amendment such as vermiculite, peat moss, or perlite. These have no fertilizer value, but they improve soil structure. Manure does both.

Lonicera japonica　　　　　　　**2-3' x 3-4'**
Japanese Honeysuckle　　　　　　**Zone 5**

Evergreen shrub in the family Caprifoliaceae native to the Orient.

Characteristics. This is a rather rampant-growing shrub, and depending on the variety, it may take on a vinelike growth habit. One of the more common landscape forms is L. j. Purpurea (with purple leaves). Most shrubby forms have very fragrant flowers, one of their main attributes. Flower color varies from white to yellow to red and combinations of all three.

Culture. These plants will grow almost anywhere but appreciate good soil preparation. Plant 2½ feet apart. It is usually best to confine this plant to a given area as it may become a pest.

Leatherleaf mahonia (top), Mahonia fortunei (bottom).

Japanese honeysuckle (top). Closeup of flowers (bottom).

Mahonia bealei　　　　　　　**7' x 4'**
Leatherleaf Mahonia　　　　　**Zone 7**

Evergreen shrub native to the Orient in the family Berberidaceae.

Characteristics. A coarse-textured, rather leggy plant with grayish-green foliage and spiny margins. Yellow flowers are produced in the spring followed by large grayish-blue berries.

Culture. This is a shrub for shaded or partially shaded areas. It appreciates a sandy acid soil; periodic removal of older canes clear to the soil line will encourage more new growth and reduce the leggy tendency of this plant. Plant 2½ feet apart.

Remarks. This is one of many species of Mahonia that could be used in a breeding program to produce a number of outstanding hybrid shrubs for southern gardens. Others include M. lomariifolia, M. trifoliolata, M. fortunei, and M. aquifolium.

Varieties. Though it's a species and not a variety, M. aquifolium, the Oregon grape holly, native to the northwestern United States, is used in the upper South to zones 6 and 7 and to some degree in the lower South. A number of varieties of this plant, including compact forms, have been selected. M. Aquifolium should contribute a great deal to a breeding program with Mahonias.

M. fortunei is also well-adapted to use in the shade and is hardy to zone 8.

Mahonia lomariifolia	**8-12′ x 3-5′**
Burmese Mahonia	**Zone 8**

Evergreen shrub in the family Berberidaceae native to China.

Characteristics. A rather upright-growing plant, not as coarse-textured as the leatherleaf mahonia, very useful in southern landscapes. Light yellow flowers and bluish-black berries are somewhat ornamental.

Culture. This plant will stand a little more sun than the leatherleaf mahonia but still needs to be in partial sun or in a shaded area. Prune out older canes each year to force new growth. Not adapted to tight soils. Plant 2½-3 feet apart.

Mahonia trifoliolata (Berberis)	**7′ x 6-8′**
Agarita	**Zone 7**

Evergreen shrub native to the southern United States in the family Berberidaceae.

Spiney-leaved foliage of agarita.

Characteristics. Spiny-leaved dense shrub with grayish-green foliage. It produces many single yellow flowers that are intensely fragrant, very attractive to bees, and followed by bright red berries which make a delicious jelly.

Culture. This plant requires good drainage, full sun, and does best in a slightly alkaline soil. It deserves more attention in southern nurseries and landscapes. Plant 3 feet apart.

Varieties. A very similar species, M. swaseyi is rather rare and is distinguished mainly by its greater number of leaflets.

Malpighia glabra	**3-10′ x 3-8′**
Barbados Cherry	**Zone 9**

Tender evergreen shrub native to the southwestern United States and South America in the family Malpighiaceae.

Characteristics. A beautiful evergreen shrub with glossy foliage, wavy in texture. It produces single pink flowers followed by red berries. This berry can be used to make jelly if you want something unusual to make jelly out of.

Culture. It will grow in almost any soil and does well in full sun or light shade. Plant 2-3 feet apart. Can also be sheared regularly to produce a ground-cover effect.

Remarks. In its northern range (upper zone 9) it often sustains freeze damage but comes back quickly in the spring. One of the most tolerant of all shrubs to extremes in growing conditions. It's called the vitamin pill tree in Florida because of the high vitamin C content of the fruit.

Barbados cherry—glossy foliage, pink flowers.

Michelia Figo (fuscata)　　　　**15' x 8-10'**
Banana Shrub　　　　　　　　　　　**Zone 8**

Evergreen shrub or small tree native to China in the family Magnoliaceae.

Characteristics. A beautiful magnolia-like shrub with smaller leaves and finer texture that produces yellow magnolia-like flowers with a distinct banana fragrance. This fragrance is most pronounced on warm evenings or if the blossoms are warmed up by holding them in hand. The plant is typically propagated by cuttings, as the seeds usually will not germinate.

Banana shrub, with leaves and flowers similar to those of the magnolia. Flowers have a fragrance similar to bananas.

Southern wax myrtle as a shrub (top), and a tree (bottom).

Culture. The banana shrub requires growing conditions similar to those of the magnolia: sandy acid soil, rich in organic matter. However, like the magnolia, it will tolerate tight, black soils if mulched and planted slightly high in an area that is well drained. It does best where it gets full sun or morning sun with afternoon shade. Plant 6 feet apart.

Myrica cerifera　　　　　**15-30' x 10-15'**
Southern Wax Myrtle　　　　　　　**Zone 7**

Evergreen to semi-evergreen shrub native to the southern United States in the family Myricaceae.

Characteristics. A very tough, big, green shrub that can be sheared and would make a good replacement for ligustrum. It has finer-textured foliage which is aromatic and sometimes used for culinary purposes.

Culture. Southern wax myrtle will grow in wet soils, dry soils, sandy soils and clay soils. It is adapted to sun or partial shade and is tolerant of salt conditions.

Remarks. There are both male and female plants in this species. The females produce grayish-green to blue, wax-covered berries that are used to produce bayberry candles.

Myrtus communis　　　　　**3-15' x 2-8'**
Common Myrtle　　　　　　　　　　**Zone 9**

Tender evergreen shrub in the family Myrtaceae native to the Mediterranean.

Characteristics. Very attractive evergreen foliage making a dense shrub. Foliage has the added features of being very aromatic as well as glossy green. Pretty white flowers are followed by purple berries.

Culture. Tolerant of most soils but likes good drainage. Does best in full sun. Plant 2-3 feet apart.

Varieties. A number of varieties have been developed, including dwarf forms (1½-2 feet) as well as variegated forms and forms with different textured foliage.

Nandina domestica   **8' x 4'**
Heavenly Bamboo   **Zone 7**

Evergreen shrub native to Asia in the family Berberidaceae.

Characteristics. Will grow in sun or shade but develops its best reddish foliage color when in at least half sun. Nandina seems to prefer afternoon sun. White flowers in the spring are not especially showy but are noticeable and are followed by red berries. A white-berried form, N. domestica Alba, is reported.

Culture. This plant is easy to grow in almost any soil. It seems to have few, if any, insect or disease pests and its main requirement is proper pruning. To ensure that the plants are full and not leggy, prune out as much as one third of the older canes at ground level each spring. This will promote continuous new sprouting from the base and a thick, dense shrub. If plants are lopped off waist-high, as is often the case, they soon become leggy and awkward-looking. Plant 2-3 feet apart.

Varieties. Several dwarf varieties have been developed, including N. domestica compacta, 3 feet high; N. domestica nana, 1½ feet high; and N. domestica pygmaea, 1 foot high. Plant 12-18 inches apart.

Nerium oleander   **20' x 10-15'**
Oleander   **Zone 9**

Evergreen shrub or small tree native to the Mediterranean in the family Apocynaceae.

Characteristics. A large flowering shrub or small tree with long leaves and dull green foliage. Flowers are white, pink, reddish-purple to bright red. Double varieties have been developed. The flowers are usually 2 inches across and there are especially fragrant varieties (often sold as "N. indicum" or "N. odorum").

Culture. Oleanders appreciate good drainage and must have full sun to bloom well. They are not heavy feeders, and too much nitrogen may produce excessive growth at the expense of flowering. They are only rarely damaged by pests such as aphids and these can easily be controlled with insecticides. A wart-like gall may sometimes form on the stems and must be pruned out and destroyed. Oleanders are very salt tolerant. Plant 4-6 feet apart.

Remarks. Oleanders make spectacular small trees, but they do require persistence in training them to this form. A stake is usually placed next to one of the stems and all leaf growth originating

Heavenly bamboo.

Oleander (top) with flowers (bottom).

from the base of the plant is removed to form a single-trunked specimen. All parts of the oleander are very poisonous if eaten. The oleander is quite salt-tolerant and so is a good choice for coastal areas.

Varieties. A number of varieties have been developed including Betty, single pink flowers; Cardinal Red, very hardy; Connie, single red; Mrs. George Roeding, double salmon-pink; Pink Double, large double pink; Red Double, red double; Tammy, bronze-red; White Single, white.

Some of the more useful new dwarf varieties are available too—Petite Pink and Petite Salmon. They may be more frost-sensitive but are valuable in lower zones 8 and 9.

Osmanthus fragrans	15-30' x 10-20'
Sweet Olive	**Zone 8**

Semi-evergreen shrub native to Asia in the family Oleaceae.

Characteristics. A rather open plant with coarse-textured foliage and small but intensely fragrant white flowers.

Culture. This plant grows best in a sandy acid soil. It will tolerate clay soils if it has good drainage. Does best in partial shade but will grow in sun if planted in good soil. Plant 6 feet apart.

Remarks. The flowers of sweet olive can be used to add a fragrant scent to tea.

Varieties. O. heterophyllus (false holly) is hardy to zone 7 and a native of Japan and Taiwan. It has holly-like foliage with spines along the leaf margins and is most frequently seen in its variegated form. It makes a beautiful, dense plant in the nursery but often becomes scraggly when planted in the landscape.

O. Fortunei is a hybrid between O. fragrans and O. heterophyllus. It looks holly-like (except for opposite rather than alternate leaves) and is less fragrant than sweet olive. It is a large plant—15 feet tall and almost as spreading (6-8 feet).

Philadelphus x virginalis	6-8' x 5'
Mock Orange	**Zone 5**

Deciduous shrub in family Saxifragaceae. A hybrid of unknown origin.

Mock orange. Fragrant white blossoms are produced in late spring.

Characteristics. An open-growing shrub with a fountain-like growth habit. It is noted mostly for its beautiful and often fragrant white blossoms which are produced in late spring.

Culture. Tolerant of most soils, it prefers a sandy, well-drained soil and although it will grow in shade, it will bloom best in full sun to light shade. Plant 3 feet apart.

Varieties. There are a great many species and varieties of mock orange native to the Americas as well as to Asia and Europe. Because of the great many hybrids, there is considerable confusion as to species. The most common species are P. coronarius and P. Lewisii.

Photinia x Fraseri	20' x 10-15'
Fraser's Photinia	**Zone 7**

Hybrid evergreen shrub in the family Rosaceae.

Characteristics. A coarse-textured shrub with bright red new growth. It also produces clusters of white flowers. If the plants are pruned regularly, these flowers probably will not form.

Culture. Tolerant to almost all soils and growing conditions except bad drainage. Produces its best foliage color in full sun, but will grow in partial shade. Plant 4 feet apart.

Fraser's photinia.

Unfortunately, in the last few years a number of reports of dieback have been coming in from around the South. The disease organism is apparently *Pellicularia* and there is no practical control except to replace these plants with a different plant, like nandina. It occurs mainly on older plants but new plants used for replacement soon die, too. Plant 4 feet apart for dense screens; 12 to 15 feet for more open specimens.

Pittosporum is rather salt-tolerant and thus is useful in coastal areas. Wheeler's pittosporum (below) is rather susceptible to leaf spot when planted in the shade.

Varieties. There is now a dwarf variety, Wheeler's pittosporum (9 feet tall; space 2½ feet apart) which has the standard green foliage. The variegated pittosporum (3 feet) has a grayish-green effect. Variegated pittosporum is slower growing if not ultimately as large as the standard green variety. It is a mainstay of southern landscapes and very much deserves its popularity. A great many other pittosporum species exist and deserve trial in southern gardens.

Powdery mildew may be a problem. Treat with karathane. Root rot and fire blight can also be a problem.

Varieties. Fraser's photinia is a hybrid of P. glabra and P. serrulata. The Japanese photinia, P. glabra, is often grown in the South. It does not have as brilliant a foliage color; it is more of a light bronze. P. serrulata is very attractive, with large leaves and prominent serrations, but it's extremely susceptible to powdery mildew and its use in the humid South is not recommended.

Green pittosporum (top), variegated pittosporum (bottom).

Pittosporum Tobira   18' x 15'
Pittosporum   **Zone 8**

Evergreen shrub native to the Orient in the family Pittosporaceae.

Characteristics. An easily grown evergreen shrub. One of the main drawbacks of this plant is that the standard varieties can become extremely large. Leaves are about 4 inches long, leathery, and the flowers, though not spectacular, are noticeable and very fragrant.

Culture. This plant is relatively easy to grow. It does best in full sun but will tolerate some shade.

Podocarpus macrophyllus
Japanese Yew

45' x 5-10'

Zone 8

Narrow evergreen shrub or tree native to the Orient in the family Podocarpaceae.

Characteristics. A narrow, exclamation point-type of plant used as a shrub but maturing into a very large tree pointed at its top. It has dark bluish-green foliage, lanceolate leaves 3-5 inches in length. There are separate male and female plants, the female plants producing a bright blue berry.

Japanese yew.

Culture. A beautiful purple aphid will sometimes attack plants, causing a sticky honeydew upon which a black sooty mold can grow. It is easily controlled with insecticides. Sometimes plants mysteriously begin to decline, turn yellow, and eventually die.

The Japanese yew likes an acid soil; optimizing growth conditions with soil acidifiers and enriching the soil with organic matter plus mulching with pine bark during the summer may help to reduce this mysterious disease problem. Plant 3 feet apart.

Varieties. Podocarpus Nagi, with larger leaflets, is useful in zone 9.

Poncirus trifoliata
Trifoliate Orange

30' x 15'

Zone 7

Deciduous shrub or small tree in the family Rutaceae native to China and related to edible citrus species.

Characteristics. Though this plant's most notable use is as a rootstock for citrus, it does have ornamental value. It makes a very interesting, if somewhat thorny, small flowering tree which produces ornamental fruit. It can also be used to make an impenetrable hedge with beautiful glossy green foliage during the summer and green thorns and stems so dense it almost appears evergreen in the winter.

Culture. This plant is very easy to grow in almost any soil and is generally grown from seed. The seeds are polyembryonic—it only takes a small handful to get a great number of plants from each seed.

Unfortunately, trifoliate orange is not offered much in the nursery trade, though nurseries dealing in citrus may have it available for rootstock or plants may occasionally sprout up after the top of a grafted citrus dies. Space 2 feet apart for a hedge, 4 feet for specimen use.

Remarks. The flowers are very fragrant and the fruit has a strong citrus fragrance. Spider mites may be a serious problem. Control them with a spray of kelthane.

Prunus caroliniana
Cherry Laurel

20-40' x 10-20'

Zone 7

Evergreen shrub or small tree in the family Rosaceae native to the southern United States.

Characteristics. Glossy green foliage is this plant's main attribute. It makes a good, large hedge but is bad about springing up all over the neighborhood from berries "planted" by the birds. Often short-lived.

Culture. Tolerant of most soils. In alkaline soils, however, it may require foliar (leaf) applications of iron chelate. See page 16. It appreciates an acid soil built up with lots of organic matter. Borers may be a problem. Spray the trunk with lindane (if available) as a preventative in April and July. Space 4-6 feet apart.

Varieties. P. Laurocerasus, the English cherry laurel, is also commonly cultivated in the East and it, too, is hardy to zone 7. Cultivars of this species have been introduced in the nursery trade.

Punica Granatum
Pomegranate

15-25' x 10-15'

Zone 8

Evergreen shrub native to southern Europe and Asia in the family Punicaceae.

Characteristics. Beautiful glossy green foliage and orange-red flowers with crinkled petals, plus edible fruit (on some varieties), give this plant considerable appeal.

Culture. It is tolerant of alkaline soils and yet will grow well in slightly acid soils. High humidity may be responsible for lack of fruitfulness in the southeastern United States, but some varieties are grown for their ornamental flowers only, while others may require cross pollination. Plant 4-6 feet apart. Dwarf varieties are excellent container plants.

Varieties. Many varieties have been introduced, including dwarf forms, white-flowered forms, and non-fruiting forms such as Chico.

The variety 'Wonderful' is often sold but is a poor fruiting variety along the Gulf Coast.

Pyracantha Koidzumii 12' x 4-8'
Fire Thorn **Zone 8**

Evergreen shrub native to the Orient in the family Rosaceae.

Characteristics. This form usually produces red fruit and is restricted to the South. The more common species, P. coccinea, is also used in the South and is hardy to zone 7. The coccinea species includes a great many varieties, many of which include Koidzumii as one of the parents.

Culture. Fire thorns are easy to grow in most soils. They flower and fruit best in full sun but will grow in partial shade. They have several major pests.

Since they belong to the rose family, they are susceptible to fire blight, a bacterial disease that can be devastating. It is best controlled with a cop-

per fungicide or an agricultural antibiotic spray during blooming. Other pests include lace bugs, spider mites, and leaf rollers. These can be controlled with general purpose insecticides. Plant 4 feet apart.

Remarks. Pyracantha berries are not poisonous, as is sometimes thought, but in fact can be used to make a delicious jelly if you have the patience to harvest them—or the opportunity before the birds get them.

Varieties. A number of dwarf varieties exist as well as varieties with more compact forms than the often scraggly common form. Plants with red or orange berries are available as are those pretrained as espalier plants for use against walls.

Raphiolepis indica 3-5' x 3'
Indian Hawthorn **Zone 8**

Evergreen flowering shrub native to China in the family Rosaceae.

Indian hawthorn, flowers (top) and fruit (bottom).

Pyracantha with the familiar orange-red berries that are its trademark.

Characteristics. Glossy green foliage and white or pink flowers are the attractions of this plant species. Most flowers are produced in early spring and are followed by black berries in the fall.

Culture. Indian hawthorn appreciates a well prepared soil and raised beds, especially where the existing soil is tight or the drainage is poor. Incorporation of organic matter such as pine bark or peat moss is recommended. These plants are often planted in too much shade or where there is poor air circulation, which fosters a leaf spot disease. This disease is always more prevalent where the plants are under stress; thus good cultural practices are important in preventing this disease. Plant 2½ feet apart.

Varieties. Many varieties of R. indica have been introduced. Some of the more popular include Apple Blossom, pink flowers; Enchantress, pink flowers, dwarf growth habit, (2 feet); Flamingo, pink flowers, medium size; Jack Evans, pink flowers, compact growth (2 feet); Pink Cloud, pinkish-red flowers, compact growth (2 feet).

In addition, R. umbellata (R. ovata) or Yedda hawthorn (3-4 feet), is sometimes offered. This plant is taller-growing (6-10 feet in height) with grayish-green foliage. Hybrids of the two species are also reported.

Rhamnus caroliniana   **30' x 15'**
Carolina Buckthorn (Indian Cherry)   **Zone 6**

Deciduous shrub or small tree in the Buckthorn family, Rhamnaceae.

Carolina buckthorn, a highly adaptable shrub or small tree.

Characteristics. A large, coarse-textured shrub most valued for its adaptability to many growing conditions and its red fruit which is early to show color in the fall.

Culture. This plant is tolerant of most soils if planted high and given good drainage. Plant 6-8 feet apart.

Remarks. Although the fruit is initially red, it eventually turns black when ripe.

Rhododendron

The genus Rhododendron includes what are typically thought of as rhododendrons: plants with larger leaves (6-8 inches in length) and glossy green, plus plants more commonly referred to as azaleas. Most of the southern species of azaleas are

Azaleas in full bloom (top). They lend an old-fashioned, fancy look to this latticework (bottom).

Azaleas: A Beautiful Southern Tradition

Successful cultivation of azaleas in the South depends primarily on (1) selection of the proper planting exposure and (2) proper planting techniques and (3) selection of varieties or species adapted to local conditions.

Most azaleas require at least partial shade, particularly during the afternoon. For this reason, north or east exposures are the safest. This isn't to say that a west or south exposure is out of the question. A lot depends on whether you have partial shade from trees (preferably deep-rooted), shrubs, or fences, screens, etc. Disaster is imminent when you plant a row of azaleas next to a brick wall with an unfiltered west exposure.

Planting technique is the most important factor. Plopping a poor azalea into gumbo soil and forgetting it usually results in failure. The best solution is to plant in raised beds where drainage is less than excellent. Till the soil 2-3 inches deep and work in sulfur at a rate of 1 lb. per 100 square feet plus superphosphate at 6-8 lbs. per 100 square feet if the soil hasn't been previously fertilized with phosphorus. If roots are matted around the outside of the soil ball, cut this mat in at least four places along its length. This will encourage the root system to branch out into the surrounding soil.

Set the soil ball 2-3 inches deep into the tilled soil and then build up a soil mix around it consisting of one part pine bark or peat moss, one part sand, calcined clay or perlite, and one part good loam topsoil. Rough cedar makes an attractive and economical form for these beds. (If you have a sandy well-drained soil you can probably plant in it if you add organic matter.)

Set the beds 2-3 inches high and have the soil tested yearly. Finally, place a 2-3 inch mulch of pine needles, pine bark, etc. on top of the soil mix and maintain this depth throughout the year. Azaleas have shallow root systems and thus don't like cultivation; this mulch will discourage weeds and maintain an even moisture content in the soil.

If these two requirements—proper exposure and soil preparation—are met, azaleas are not difficult to grow in the South.

Possible problems include:

Azalea Petal Blight: Symptoms—blooms become soft and collapse. Control—clean up old dead flowers and spray blooms with a fungicide.

Leaf Blotch and Twig Blight: Symptoms—bronzed leaves, excessive leaf drop, and small black fruiting bodies on the leaf lesions. Control—plant in a favorable environment; spray with a copper fungicide such as Kocide 101.

Root Rot: Symptoms—growth is retarded, leaves on one or more branches turn gray-green, followed by wilting and finally death. Control—avoid planting in low wet places, plant in raised beds.

Insect Pests: Control—malathion or dimethoate will control most insect pests on azaleas.

Some other good practices to follow: fertilize with an acid fertilizer (often called azalea food) immediately after bloom and 4-6 weeks later. Have the soil tested yearly. You may find sulfur or iron sulfate (copperas) necessary every year at 1 lb. per 100 square feet.

Water during a dry winter as well as in the summer (July and August are particularly critical months because azaleas are setting buds).

Varieties (Numerous—these are just some suggestions):

WHITE
Glacier
Mrs. G.G. Gerbing
Gumpo (late)
Fielder's White
King's White

VIOLET
Formosa
George Lindley Taber

PINK
Snow
Judge Soloman
Pink Ruffles
Coral Bells
Daphne Salmon
Fashion
Sweetheart Supreme
Macrantha (late)
Wild Azalea (Rhododendron canescens)

RED
President Clay
Christmas Cheer
Hinodegiri

evergreen; however, there are deciduous native species.

The brilliant yellow and orange flowers of the Ghent hybrids are not adapted to the lower, humid South. Most of the cultivated varieties offered in the southern nurseries come from one of the following groups: the Indica hybrids from R. indicum, R. Simsii, and R. mucronatum; Kaempferi hybrids developed from R. Kaempferi; Kurume hybrids developed from R. Kaempferi and R. Kiusianum.

Some of the most notable native southern azaleas which deserve increased cultivation (though they are often a bit scraggly and deciduous) include R. alabamense (white with a yellow blotch, fragrant flowers, zone 7); R. austrinum, or Florida flame azalea (small yellow blooms, fragrant, hardy to zone 6); R. oblongifolium (deciduous, white flowers, zone 7); R. canescens (deciduous, to 15 feet, flowers pink to white, zone 7); R. serrulatum (deciduous, to 20 feet, flowers after leaves appear, white and fragrant, zone 7).

These species should be experimented with to give southerners better adapted azaleas with the same outstanding features of the imported varieties.

Rhus copallina   15′ x 8′
Flameleaf Sumac   **Zone 5**

Deciduous shrub in the family Anacardiaceae native to the eastern United States.

Characteristics. Sumacs are rarely offered for use in the landscape but they do have certain characteristics that recommended them. Some produce ornamental seed heads, but by far the most important characteristic is their brilliant red fall color.

Culture. Sumacs will grow in almost any soil, from sand to clay, and are tolerant of both wet and dry conditions depending on the species. Plant 4 feet apart.

Remarks. Poison sumac (R. Vernix) and poison ivy (R. radicans) belong to this genus. You won't find them for sale though.

Varieties. Several species of Rhus need to be used more, including R. glabra, the smooth Sumac, and R. aromatica, fragrant Sumac. In addition, several Asian species are of interest.

Sophora secundiflora   20-40′ x 10-20′
Mescal Bean Sophora   **Zone 8**

Evergreen shrub native to the southwestern United States in the family Leguminosae.

Characteristics. This is a beautiful, large evergreen native American shrub. It produces dark purple, wisteria-like blossoms that are intensely fragrant and reminiscent of grape soda. It's main drawback is that it also produces large orange seeds which are poisonous. However, they are en-

Mescal bean sophora produces purple blossoms reminiscent of wisteria.

Flameleaf sumac growing wild in its native setting.

cased in a tough, woody seed pod and would take some persistence on the part of youngsters to get at them. So many plants are poisonous, it would be unfair to eliminate this plant from our landscapes for this one feature alone.

Culture. This sophora is rather slow-growing and does best in full sun, with good drainage and a neutral to alkaline soil. In sandy acid soil regions, mixing 5 lbs. of lime per 100 square feet of planting bed is beneficial. Plant 8 feet apart.

Ternstroemia gymnanthera 8' x 6'
(Cleyera japonica) **Zone 8**

An evergreen shrub of the Theaceae family.

Characteristics. A beautiful glossy foliaged evergreen shrub with burgundy red new growth. Gives a very tropical appearance.

Culture. Although in the same family as camellia, this plant is more tolerant of soil types. It too appreciates an acid soil and raised beds which have been built up with the incorporation of two inches of peat moss or pine bark plus topsoil and sand in a similar amount. Acid fertilizers, such as azalea-camellia food, are also helpful, and if iron chlorosis is a problem, foliar sprays of iron chelate will be beneficial. Plant 3 feet apart in sun or partial shade.

Remarks. One of the most beautiful and useful plants for the South. Even though commonly planted, its many attributes make it worth planting everywhere.

Varieties. This plant is often mistakenly sold as Cleyera japonica, which does exist but is only rarely available in the nursery trade. Cleyera has larger leaves.

Ternstroemia gymnanthera.

Viburnum dentatum 12' x 5'
Arrowwood Viburnum **Zone 3**

Deciduous shrub native to the United States in the family Caprifoliaceae.

Characteristics. A rather open shrub of value for naturalizing in partially shaded shrub borders. White flowers and attractive foliage are its main attributes.
Tree forms and big-leaved forms are found in East Texas.

Culture. Grows best in sandy, moist soils. Often found as an understory plant; it is tolerant of partial shade. Plant 3 feet apart.

Viburnum japonicum 10' x 10'
Japanese Viburnum **Zone 7**

Coarse-textured evergreen shrub in the family Caprifoliaceae.

Characteristics. This shrub serves much the same purpose as waxleaf ligustrum, being a dense, coarse-textured evergreen. It is relatively insect- and disease-free.

Culture. Grows under almost any soil conditions in sun or partial shade. Plant 4 feet apart.

Varieties. V. odoratissimum, sweet viburnum, is very similar and is often confused with Japanese viburnum. It has fragrant white flowers and may grow to 12 feet in height. It rarely blooms, and it is more upright and has oily-textured banes compared to sweet Viburnum.

Viburnum nudum 15' x 10'
Black Alder (Possumhaw Viburnum) **Zone 7**

Semi-evergreen shrub native to the southern United States in the family Caprifoliaceae.

Characteristics. A coarse-textured shrub of value for its bronzy fall color.

Culture. Tolerant of wet soils and well adapted to the South. Plant 3-4 feet apart.

(From left to right): arrow wood viburnum, Japanese viburnum, black alder, and sandankwa viburnum.

Remarks. This plant is, unfortunately, rarely offered in the nursery trade, but deserves more attention.

V. nitidum is a small-leaved variety, more compact and red in the fall. It is rarely offered in the nursery trade.

V. acerifolium, maple-leafed viburnum, also deserves increased use even though it has been cultivated for centuries and several varieties have been described. It has dark purple fall color.

Viburnum suspensum	6' x 4-6'
Sandankwa Viburnum	Zone 8

Evergreen shrub native to the Ryukyu Islands (Southeast Asia) in the family Caprifoliaceae.

Characteristics. A rough-leaved evergreen viburnum, much used in southern landscapes, which produces pink flowers in the spring. The flowers are fragrant, almost sickeningly so.

Culture. Easily grown in most soils, the plants appreciate amendment with organic matter and are adapted to sun or partial shade. Plant 3 feet apart.

Viburnum Tinus (Laurustinus)	4-10' x 6'
Roundleaf Viburnum	Zone 7

Evergreen shrub native to the Mediterranean in the family Caprifoliaceae.

Characteristics. A commonly used evergreen shrub in southern landscapes. There are many varieties which produce either white or pinkish flowers that are somewhat ornamental and fragrant.

Culture. Adapted to most soils but appreciate prepared beds. Roundleaf can be grown in sun or partial shade. Plant 3 feet apart.

Varieties. Dwarf varieties are offered in nurseries.

Xylosma congestum (senticosa)	15' x 8'
Xylosma	Zone 9

An evergreen shrub native to China in the family Flacourtiaceae.

Characteristics. This is an evergreen shrub valued for its bronzy new growth and as a barrier plant for its small spines.

Culture. Easily grown in most soils, it appreciates good drainage and a prepared bed. Will grow in full sun or partial shade; however, it develops its best foliage color in full sun. Has few pests. Plant 4-6 feet apart.

Remarks. This is a most useful plant. It can be pruned to a small specimen tree form. Xylosma is perhaps the most typical "shrub"—in form and appearance—one can find.

A Guide to Southern Vines

Antigonon leptopus　　　　　　　　40'
Coral Vine (Mexican Creeper)　　　**Zone 8**

Deciduous vine of the family Polygonaceae native to Mexico and Central America.

Characteristics. A rank-growing vine of value mainly for its bright pink flowers produced in late summer or early fall. There is also a white-flowered form, though it is relatively rare and less hardy. Reportedly, plants in tropical areas produce edible tubers.

Culture. This vine will grow almost anywhere. It is ideally suited to an area where a large amount of dense growth is needed for privacy. Plant 12 feet apart.

Varieties. Cv. album, with white flowers, is available.

Coral vine.

Asarina (Maurandya) antirrhinifolia　　5'
Snapdragon Vine　　　　　　　　　**Zone 8**

Deciduous vine in the family Scrophulariaceae native to the southwestern United States and Mexico.

Characteristics. Produces purple or white blossoms with yellow throats, similar to snapdragons.

Culture. This plant does best where it has a limey soil and good drainage. Therefore, incorporation of 5 lbs. of agricultural limestone or dolomitic limestone is advisable in a raised planting bed.

Bignonia capreolata (Anisostichus　　50'
capreolatus)　　　　　　　　　**Zone 7**
Cross Vine

Evergreen woody vine in the family Bignoniaceae. Native to the southeastern United States.

Cross vine.

Characteristics. This is a much neglected vine in southern landscapes. It is especially valuable both for its evergreen foliage which takes on a purplish hue in the winter and its beautiful spring flowers. The flowers are trumpet-shaped, usually have a yellow-to-cinnamon color, are very fragrant and attractive to bees. This vine can be grown further north, probably to zone 6, where it is roothardy.

Culture. Cross Vine grows in wet, often swampy, areas where there is a sandy, acid soil. Thus, although it does not *require* poor drainage, it is somewhat tolerant of wet soils for short periods of time and it appreciates an acid soil. Incorporation of several inches of pine bark or peat moss into the soil prior to planting is advisable. Also, 1-2 lbs. of sulfur per 100 square feet worked in with the soil will be beneficial. The vine is best adapted to sun and is often seen growing up old cottonwood trees. It can be started in partial shade and allowed to climb to a sunny location. Plant 8 feet apart.

Varieties. B. capreolata atrosanguinea is a variety reported to have long narrow leaves and darker-colored flowers.

Bougainvillea hybrida	**15-20'**
Bougainvillea	**Zone 9**

Evergreen vine of the family Nyctaginaceae native to Mexico and South America.

Characteristics. Bougainvillea produces beautiful, papery, bright-colored bracts and small insignificant flowers. The bracts are very long-lasting and showy.

Bougainvillea produces brightly colored bracts from white to purple.

Culture. Bougainvillea is only semi-hardy in zone 9, but will usually come back even if slightly frozen when located in a protected area. Its main disadvantage is that it grows so well in high rainfall areas that it sometimes forgets to bloom. Root pruning, by taking a spade and pushing it into the soil about 24 inches from the base of the plant all around, may help. Growing the plants in pots or hanging baskets sometimes helps to promote blooming too. Use of a low nitrogen fertilizer (for instance, 6-24-24) also helps by reducing vegetative growth and promoting flowering.

The plants grow best in a neutral-to-alkaline soil. In sandy acid soils or in potting soils a small amount of lime may be beneficial; use 5 lbs. per 100 square feet of planting bed area, or for potted plants, water the pots once with a saturated solution of lime. This is accomplished by putting 1 to 2 cups of hydrated lime in a gallon of water, stir thoroughly for about 5 minutes and allow to settle. The solution above the settled lime will contain a concentrated amount of lime and about 1 pint per pot should be sufficient. Plant 4 feet apart.

Varieties. Barbara Karst, red flowers; brasiliensis, purplish flowers, hardy; California Gold, golden-orange flowers; Orange King, bronzy-orange flowers; Convent, purple flowers; Isabel Greensmith, red flowers with golden cast; Jamaica White, white flowers shading pink; Scarlett O'Hara, red flowers, vigorous.

Campsis radicans	**25'**
Trumpet Creeper	**Zone 5**

Deciduous vine of the family Bignoniaceae native to North America and Asia.

Characteristics. A strong-growing vine producing orange-to-scarlet-colored trumpet-shaped flowers in the summer. Climbs by aerial rootlets and so can attach itself to brick.

Culture. Very easy to grow in almost any soil. Flowers best in full sun. Plant 12 feet apart.

Remarks: Flowers attract hummingbirds.

Varieties. There are several varieties, including ones that produce yellow flowers. One of the most significant varieties is Madam Galen, which is a hybrid between C. grandiflora (the Asian species) and C. radicans.

Chinese trumpet creeper.

Texas clematis.

C. grandiflora, the Chinese Trumpet Creeper, is a much superior plant, but it has been difficult to propagate, and even where hardy (to zone 8) it has not been widely grown.

Clematis texensis   **8′**
Texas Clematis   **Zone 7 (?)**

Deciduous vine in the family Ranunculaceae native to the southwestern United States.

Characteristics. This plant is primarily of value for its delicate, trumpet-like red flowers about 3/4 inch long.

Culture. Clematis is relatively easy to grow, but in sandy acid soils it appreciates some lime (about 5 lbs. per 100 square feet of bed area). Plant 3 feet apart. A heavy mulch in summer is a sure way to succeed with Clematis.

Remarks. The hybrid Clematis are often desired in southern gardens, but at least in the lower South (zone 8 and below) they are rather difficult to grow. Some varieties, such as Jackmanii (purple, white and red forms exist), Duchess of Edinburg (white, fragrant) and Henryi (white), may be grown with relative success.

Varieties. C. crispa, with light blue flowers, native to Texas and sometimes called blue jasmine, is also found but rarely planted. It nevertheless possesses the genetic potential to extend the range of hybrid clematis into the South and Southwest. Another species, C. paniculata, native to New Zealand, with white flowers, is grown to some degree and is very vigorous in the South but really is of limited value.

C. reticulata has yellowish flowers and is native to the Southeast.

Clytostoma callistegioides (Bignonia   **15-20′**
violacea)   **Zone 9**
Argentine Trumpet Vine

Tender evergreen vine in the family Bignoniaceae native to Brazil and Argentina.

Characteristics. A fast-growing vine, roothardy in Zone 9, which produces lavender to violet trumpet-like flowers.

Culture. Does well in almost any soil; best in full sun. It establishes more easily in morning sun, afternoon shade. It may freeze to the ground, but it returns each spring. Plant 8 feet apart.

Decumaria barbara   **30′**
Climbing Hydrangea   **Zone 6**

Deciduous vine of the family Saxifragaceae native to the southeastern United States.

Characteristics. A vigorous-growing half-evergreen vine which climbs with aerial rootlets and produces white, fragrant, hydrangea-like blossoms.

Culture. Does best in a sandy acid soil enriched with organic matter. Difficult to transplant and uncommon in the nursery trade. Plant 15 feet apart.

Dioscorea bulbifera
Potato Vine (Air Potato)

30'
Zone 8

Deciduous vine of the family Dioscoreaceae native to Asia.

Characteristics. A vigorous vine, technically an annual sprouting back from leathery aerial tubers or from the root system. It produces beautiful heart-shaped leaves with prominent veins.

Potato vine.

Culture. Will grow in almost any soil; sun or shade, and is of value mainly for its glossy green leaves. Plant 4-6 feet apart.

Remarks. There are edible forms of this plant, though the commonly planted varieties may be toxic and should not be consumed. The chief means of propagation is by the leathery tubers which are usually passed from friend to friend. It is a valuable vine for its strong growth and tropical appearance.

Ficus pumila
Climbing Fig (Creeping Fig)

50'
Zone 8

Evergreen vine in the family Moraceae native to Asia.

Characteristics. A vigorous vine. Once established, it serves the same purpose as English ivy—it climbs walls, covers the ground, etc. Mature foliage is larger than juvenile foliage. The rootlets of this vine may permanently mar brick if the plant dies or is removed.

Culture. Grows in almost any soil, in sun or shade, and rapidly covers brick walls once established.

Creeping fig.

May grow slowly the first season. Plant 4 feet apart.

Varieties. A small-leaved variety, F. pumila minima, is offered. However, as the plant matures, leaves become larger. An available variegated form is very attractive for hanging baskets and can be used in the landscape as well. The variegation is rather striking, a clean white on green. The variegated variety is less vigorous.

Gelsemium sempervirens
Carolina Jasmine, Jessamine
(Evening Trumpet Flower)

15-20'
Zone 8

Semi-evergreen vine in the family Loganiaceae native to the southern United States.

Characteristics. This is another strong-growing vine primarily valued because of its bright yellow trumpet-like flowers in the early spring. Flowers are also fragrant. The vine is semi-evergreen and

Carolina jessamine.

gives some privacy during winter, however the foliage may thin out and take on a bronzy color by early spring.

The plant is extremely poisonous, but this should be a relatively minor consideration when deciding on plants, since so many are poisonous.

Culture. Grows best in a sandy acid soil but is relatively tolerant of soil types and can be used almost anywhere. Flowers best in full sun, but will grow in partial shade. Plant 3-4 feet apart.

Hedera canariensis   **30'**
Algerian Ivy   **Zone 8**

Evergreen vine of the family Araliaceae native to Europe, the Canary Islands, and North Africa.

Characteristics. This is a large-leafed, more tender form of the common English ivy, H. helix, that is very useful in the south as a groundcover or as a climbing vine. This plant is perhaps a little easier to grow than English ivy.

Culture. Grows in almost any soil, but likes a little moisture. Both species are susceptible to a "summer disease" which is caused by *rhizoctonia* fungus. Sprays of benomyl during late spring and early summer with emphasis put on placing the material at the stem line will help to control this disease. Plant 2-3 feet apart.

Varieties. H. helix (English ivy) and its many forms can also be grown in the South but are best adapted to shaded locations.

There are many forms of both varieties, more so of H. helix than of the Algerian ivy. These varieties consist of variegated forms and, in the case of English ivy, forms which vary in the number of leaves and the curled or crinkled texture of the foliage.

Fatshedera lizei is a shrubby vine sometimes referred to as "Botanical Wonder" because of its bigeneric parentage: Hedera X Fatsia. It is hardy to zone 8.

Lonicera sempervirens   **10-15'**
Trumpet Honeysuckle   **Zone 4**

Evergreen vine in the family Caprifoliaceae native to the United States from Connecticut to Texas.

Characteristics. An evergreen vine in the South, not nearly as rambunctious in growth as the Asiatic species of honeysuckle, it is of primary value for its red, trumpet-like flowers which attract hummingbirds.

Culture. Will grow in almost any soil and needs some type of trellis for support. Plant 4 feet apart.

Varieties. Many species of honeysuckle can be grown in the South. Some, such as L. japonica, are almost too vigorous to be considered. But the latter, at least, is of value for its extremely fragrant yellow and white flowers. If confined to a restricted soil bed area—where a sidewalk or driveway borders a narrow planting space, for example—it can be extremely useful.

Trumpet honeysuckle.

Algerian ivy.

Algerian Ivy, Trumpet Honeysuckle   55

Macfadyena (Doxanthus)
Unguis-Cati
Cat's-claw (Funnel Creeper)

80-100′
Zone 9, root-
hardy zone 8

Tender evergreen vine in the family Bignonia-ceae native to Mexico, Central and South America.

Characteristics. The picture of a beautiful, huge oak tree in full bloom with magnificent yellow flowers sticks in my mind when I think of this plant because it was actually this vine that had climbed 60 or 70 feet into the tree and bloomed. This gives some indication of its extreme vigor. It climbs by claw-like tendrils and produces beautiful trumpet-shaped bright yellow flowers.

Passionflower.

Cat's-claw (note claw-like growth on thumb).

Culture. This vine will grow in almost any location. It does best in full sun in a protected location on the south side of the house, but even if planted in the shade, it will climb up to meet the sun. Plant 15-25 feet apart.

Passiflora caerulea
Blue Passionflower

15-25′
Zone 8

Tender evergreen vine in the family Passiflor-aceae native to South America.

Characteristics. Fast-growing vine; a tender evergreen in the tropics. Some forms withstand a certain amount of frost in lower regions of zone 8 and can be grown with considerable success. There are a number of flower colors and forms; blue

flowers seem to be the most hardy. The P. coccinea, often grown in greenhouses, is a red-flowered form that is extremely beautiful and tender.

Culture. Easily grown in almost any soil. Passionflowers are somewhat susceptible to nematodes, and where commercially cultivated the microscopic roundworms can cause crop failure. Grows best in full sun. Plant 4 feet apart.

Varieties. Many species exist. One, P. incarnata, the maypop vine, is commonly found in the southeastern United States. It has an edible fruit which is best used when completely ripe after it has dropped to the ground. The pulp can then be removed, crushed, and an excellent juice extracted for use in preparing soft drinks. The maypop has three-lobed leaves versus the five-lobed leaves of P. caerulea.

Stigmaphyllon ciliatum
Butterfly Vine

15-25′
Zone 9

Deciduous vine of the family Malpighiaceae native to Mexico, Central and South America.

Characteristics. This vine is valued for its beautiful glossy green foliage but is grown primarily for its interesting seed pods which look like three butterflies stuck together. These chartreuse seed pods are 2 inches or more in diameter. They turn tan or brown at maturity and are very striking in dried flower arrangements. The vine also produces attractive single yellow flowers.

Butterfly vine (note "wings" on seed pod in the lower photograph).

Confederate jasmine.

Culture. Best grown on the South side of a structure in zone 8 where it may be only roothardy. Butterfly vine rapidly covers a fence.

One pest to be aware of is the root knot nematode, a microscopic roundworm that attacks the root system. Sterilizing the soil with vapam prior to planting will reduce the possibility of nematode infection. Plant 4-6 feet apart.

Trachelospermum jasminoides   **15-20′**
Confederate Jasmine   **Zone 8**

Evergreen vine in the family Apocynaceae native to China.

Characteristics. One of the most useful of all southern evergreen vines, it is adapted to culture in both sun or shade, though it produces more flowers when grown in the sun. Often used to climb up lightpoles or mail boxes, it is equally valuable for its use as a screening vine. The white star-like flowers produced in the spring are extremely fragrant.

Culture. Grows in almost any soil in either shade or sun. Appreciates 2-4 inches of organic matter such as peat moss plus 2-4 lbs. of complete fertilizer such as 12-24-12 per 100 square feet in the planting bed. Plant 3-4 feet apart.

Vitis rotundifolia   **25-60′**
Muscadine Grape   **Zone 6**

Deciduous vine of the family Vitaceae native to the southeastern United States.

Characteristics. This is a vigorous vine found in its native habitat in both male and female forms. In the last few years, self-fertile varieties containing both male and female parts on the vine have been developed and are used as pollinators in addition to the pistillate, or female, forms.

Usually planted for fruit, muscadines are very ornamental as well. They have glossy green foliage, much more attractive than the European and most native American grape varieties, and the huge grape-like fruit is ornamental as well as delicious. Fall color is a bright yellow. For detailed growing information, see *Growing Fruits, Berries & Nuts in the South* by Dr. George Ray McEachern (Pacesetter Books).

Culture. Muscadines do best in a slightly acid soil (pH 6.0-6.5) enriched with organic matter. Raised beds may be necessary if poor drainage is a problem. Plant 12 feet apart.

Varieties. Self-fertile: Magnolia, amber; Carlos, amber; Southland, purple; Magoon, purple. Pistillate (female must have a self-fertile variety for pollination): Jumbo, purple; Hunt, purple; Scuppernong, amber; Fry, amber.

Wisteria sinensis	**75'**
Chinese Wisteria	**Zone 5**

Deciduous vine in the family Leguminosae native to Asia.

Characteristics. Rank-growing vine or small specimen tree producing white-to-lilac-colored, very fragrant flowers. The plants are often vigorous enough to be invasive.

Culture. Grows in almost any soil but appreciates organic matter and the addition of fertilizer. They will bloom best if planted in full sun. Excess fertilizer may prevent blooming. Root pruning is sometimes used to promote bloom. To root prune push a spade into the soil 2-3 feet from the base of the plant. Plant 15-20 feet apart.

Varieties. There are several native varieties, including W. macrostachya (zone 6, late-flowering) and W. frutescens (zone 5), which are native to the southern United States and although not as spectacular, are perhaps better adapted and are worthy of use in a breeding program to develop wisterias especially for the South. Another species, W. megasperma, the evergreen wisteria, is often used in the South. The main objection to this plant is that the flowers are such a dark purple that they are only barely noticeable. Its beautiful glossy green foliage, however, is extremely attractive.

Wisteria in full bloom (left) closeup of blooms (top right). Once you let it get out of hand, wisteria can be a problem (bottom right).

Other Shrubs for the South

Buddleia Davidii   15' x 10'
Butterfly Bush (Summer Lilac)   **Zone 5**

This deciduous shrub from China, in the family Loganiaceae, is a rather vigorous shrub with wide-spreading branches. Flowers are typically lilac, often with a contrasting yellow or orange eye in spikes 10-15 inches long. A number of varieties are listed that vary from lavender-pink to violet-blue in color.

Butterfly bush will grow in almost any soil and makes lush growth with little care. It is somewhat open and best used as an informal border planting.

Condalia hookeri

This West Texas native is valuable because of its drought tolerance and also because it always appears to have bright green, new growth. It needs full sun and good drainage to survive and appreciates lime in the soil (5 lbs. per 100 square feet), especially in acid soils.

Cyrilla racemiflora   15-20' x 10-15'
Leatherwood (TiTi)   **Zone 8**

A rather large semi-evergreen shrub (family Cyrillaceae) tolerant of soils too wet for other plants. It requires a good bit of water and thus should not be planted with more drought-tolerant species. Its chief value is its beautiful green foliage. Showy flowers produced in racemes 6 inches long are very attractive to bees.

Exochorda sp.   12-15' x 5-7'
Pearlbushes   **Zone 5**

Deciduous shrubs in the family Rosaceae not used as much as they should be in the South. Their white flowers are very ornamental. The plants prosper in full sun and well-drained soil. They will not do well near the coast since they're very salt sensitive.

Eysenhardtia texana
Kidney Wood   **Zone 8**

This is a shrub that grows well along the upper Gulf Coast and inland several hundred miles. It is valued for its periodic production of white flowers but needs pruning to maintain a dense form.

Forsythia sp.   6-10' x 3-5'
Golden-Bells   **Zones 5-7**

There are a number of Forsythia species, or Golden-Bells, that are prized for their early, brilliant yellow blooms. However, from Zone 8 south they are of limited value because of a tendency to bloom sparsely and to make rather poor growth due to long wet summers and a lack of winter chilling.

Hamamelis virginiana   15-30' x 8-12'
Witch Hazel   **Zone 5**

The Witch Hazels, including the common Witch Hazel as well as H. vernalis (to 6 feet high), H. mollis (Chinese Witch Hazel) and H. japonica (Japanese Witch Hazel), are of value mainly for their yellow flowers. The bark and leaves of H. virginiana are reported to have medicinal properties, and the yellow fall flowers are outstanding. The plant also displays excellent fall foliage color. All Witch Hazels thrive in moist soils.

Juniperus sp.   **Variable**
Juniper or Cedar   **Zones 4-7**

There are a great many species of juniper offered in the nursery trade. In the South, especially in humid areas, there is room for doubt about their general desirability in landscapes. They are typically susceptible to bagworms, spider mites, and diseases which cause defoliation and loss of needles. One only has to walk into the local nursery to find this bewildering assortment of junipers but don't be surprised if you find many of them already in various stages of decline. They are best used where good drainage and adequate air circulation can be provided.

Leitneria floridana	**25' x 12'**
Corkwood	**Zone 6**

This is a good shrub for wet places. It is not especially ornamental, but it is very tou⌐ a and easy to grow.

Litsea aestivalis	**9' x 5'**
Pondspice	**Zone 8**

An evergreen shrub with spreading growth habit in the Lauraceae family native to the southeastern United States. Another species, L. glutinosa (native to tropical Asia) is an evergreen, and it too is worthy of trial. The foliage of a Mexican species is used for seasoning in Mexico.

Loropetalum chinense	**12' x 6'**
Chinese Witch Hazel	**Zone 8**

This is an evergreen shrub which has showy white flowers. It is vigorous and easy to grow in shade or sun. Its common name is misleading; the plant is a branch of the witch hazel family (Hamamelidaceae) but, technically, Chinese witch hazel is Hamamelis mollis (page 59).

Pieris sp.	**Variable**
	Zones 5-7

The (Pieris) species (of the blueberry family, Ericaceae) have some value in the South. Their main attraction is small bell-like flowers. They are a bit finicky in their growth requirements. They need a sandy acid soil with lots of organic matter. Species include: P. floribunda, height 6 feet, native to the southeastern United States (zone 5); P. formosa, height 20 feet, native to the Himalayas (zone 7); P. forrestii, height 10 feet, native to the Himalayas (zone 7); P. japonica (lily-of-the-valley bush), height 15-30 feet native to Japan (zone 6). The latter is the most common cultivar in the nursery trade. Several varieties, including a dwarf form and a variegated form, are offered.

Rosa banksiae.

Rosa laevigata	**3-6' x 4-6'**
Cherokee Rose	**Zone 7**

This deciduous shrub of the family Rosaceae is native to China but has been naturalized in the southern U.S.

Most roses don't qualify as landscape shrubs, but newer developments with hybrids may yield some that are easy enough to care for to be considered in this category. The Cherokee Rose is an old-fashioned plant deserving of more use in the landscape. It produces large single white flowers only in the spring and is very easy to grow.

Another rose, R. banksiae, is often used in the South as a large climber. It qualifies equally as a cascading shrub. This is perhaps its best use, trailing over a wall. It can become quite large (20 feet or taller) and is completely covered with double yellow blossoms in the early spring. There is also a white-flowered form and a single yellow form, but neither of these is as common nor as floriferous as the double yellow form, Lutea.

Spiraea sp.	**6' x 4'**
	Zone 6

Spiraeas are mainstays of northern gardens, and some species are used considerably in the South, particularly the Reeve's Spiraea, S. cantoniensis. The flowering period is of short duration, and un-

Spiraea in full bloom.

Vaccinium arboreum
Tree Huckleberry (Farkleberry)

Vaccinium arboreum is a large, semi-evergreen shrub in the blueberry family (Ericaceae) desired for its show of white, bell-like flowers. It also produces a tiny edible fruit so small that one would have to be quite hungry to bother.

The Rabbiteye Blueberry, V. ashei, has been developed to a large extent for its fruit, and it too could be used in southern landscapes where the very acid soils required by most Vaccinium species exist. If selected from a *southern* source, V. myrsinites (dwarf evergreen blueberry) also has possibilities, as do other native species, many of which have brilliant burgundy red fall color. Tree huckleberry likes an acid soil (pH 4.5-6.0), a fairly moist soil, and plenty of mulch.

Tree huckleberry (top) and rabbiteye blueberry (bottom).

less a mass of early-spring white color is needed in the landscape, they are of limited value. They like full sun, rich soil, and plenty of moisture.

Styrax sp.	Variable
Snowbells	Zone 7

Styrax species are members of the family Styracaceae noted for their white, bell-like flowers. There are several American species, such as S. americanus (Mock Orange), a deciduous shrub to 10 feet hardy to zone 7, as well as tropical oriental species from which benzoin is derived.

S. texana and S. platinifolia, native to central and west Texas, are rare. In general the plants like a light, very well-drained soil.

Taxus sp.	Variable
Yews	Zone 6

Most of the true yews are not reliable in the South because they object to our long, hot, wet summers. There are a great many species and varieties, however, and no doubt some are worth trying. Podocarpus macrophyllus (Japanese Yew) is used as a substitute plant, but it is not a member of the yew family (Taxaceae); it belongs to the family Podocarpaceae.

The Japanese Yew is hardy to zone 8 and is really more a tree than a shrub, reaching 50 feet in height. It prefers soil on the dry side, and can be kept shorter by judicious pruning.

Weigela sp.　　　　　　　　6-12' x 3-6'
　　　　　　　　　　　　　　　Zone 5

Deciduous shrubs, native to Asia in the family Caprifoliaceae. The most common varieties are derived from W. florida, native to North China and Korea and hardy to Zone 5. Flowers vary from white to pink to red. There are a number of species and hybrids that deserve experimentation in the South.

Weigelas grow well in any good garden soil, kept reasonably moist, and they do appreciate a little winter protection around the base and root area in zones 6 and 7. Don't prune before flowering—blooms are borne on last year's wood.

Xanthoceras sorbifolium　　　　15' x 7'
　　　　　　　　　　　　　　　Zone 6

A deciduous shrub sometimes called "popcorn shrub" because of its large clusters of white flowers. This is an uncommon shrub of the family Sapindaceae, and it deserves more attention in southern gardens. Leaves are coarse, as much as a foot long, and the plant is robust in growth. Provide rich soil.

Xanthorhiza simplicissima　　　2' x 2'
Yellow-Root　　　　　　　　　Zone 5

A small deciduous shrub in the family Ranunculaceae native to the eastern United States and well-adapted to wet, shaded areas. Spreads by runners.

Zanthoxylum Fagara　　　　10-30' x 5-10'
Lime Prickly Ash (Wild Lime)　　Zone 7

This plant is usually a shrub in the southern United States, though in the tropics it may make a small tree. It has fine-textured evergreen leaves and numerous small thorns. This is a great shrub as a small specimen plant or for impenetrable hedges.

Winter protect in zone 7. The foliage is used as a nerve tonic and sudorific (perspiration agent).

Other Vines for the South

Calonyction aculeatum (Ipomoea alba)   30'
Moonflower Vine   **Zone 8**

This robust vine produces fragrant white flowers that open in the evening and close in daylight. It likes a rich soil and is rather easy to grow under most conditions. Moonflower is related to morning glory, which is classified in the genus Ipomoea. Authorities are divided on the correct botanical name.

Cocculus carolinus   12'
Carolina Moonseed (Red Moonseed)   **Zone 7**

A vine of the family Menispermaceae, which includes a number of plants used medicinally. This vine produces showy red berries ¼ inch in diameter. It is a relatively easy vine to grow in moist soil.

Ipomoea spp.   15'
Morning Glory   **Zone 7**

This genus includes the yam-producing sweet potato vine (I. Batatas), the common morning glory (I. pupurea), the star ipomoea (I. coccinea), and the wild potato vine (I. pandurata). All these species grow well in the South, with little care. I. Batatas and I. pandurata are perennials that grow back from tubers each year, while the other species are annuals that regrow from seed. Morning glory is useful for covering fences, trellises, walls, etc., and it flowers best in full sun. Flower colors vary: I. pupurea—pink tip, purple throat; I. coccinea—scarlet tip, yellow throat; I. pandurata—white tip, purple throat. The seeds of some species possess hallucinogenic properties.

Manettia cordifolia (Manettia glabra)   20'
Firecracker Vine   **Zone 9**

This vine is grown for its bright red summer flowers. It grows well with average moisture and soil, but it is somewhat tender and will start to die back once temperatures stay below 50-55° for any length of time.

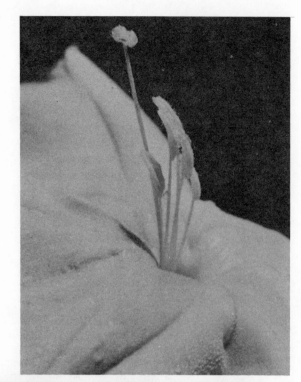

An interplanting of moonflower (top) and morning glory (bottom) would provide you with fragrant white flowers in the evening and brilliant magenta blooms in the daytime.

Old-fashioned blossoms of Thunbergia make this a perfect vine for trellises, porches, and the like. Blue- and yellow-flowered varieties are most common. Pictured here is T.g. 'alba', white-flowered variety.

Parthenocissus quinquefolia   **50′**
Virginia Creeper (Woodbine)   **Zone 4**

This hardy vine needs little attention to begin covering trellises and fences. It grows quite high and can get into trees. The bark is used medicinally. Several varieties are listed, offering variation in leaf and branching habits.

Smilax lanceolata   **25′**
Catbrier (Jackson Brier)   **Zone 8**

Tropical relatives of this evergreen vine produce the flavoring for sarsaparilla. The older stems of catbrier get a bit prickly and can be bothersome when pruning or removing. Otherwise, this is another easy vine to grow in the lower South.

Thunbergia grandiflora   **20′**
Clock Vine (Bengal Clock Vine,   **Zone 8**
Blue Trumpet Vine)

This is a popular southern vine for porches, arbors, etc. Its pretty blue flowers are quite noticeable, drooping in racemes 1-2 inches long. Thunbergia prefers a sunny exposure, rich soil, and average moisture. A white-flowered variety, T. g. 'alba' is also available.

A Spacing Guide to Southern Shrubs and Vines

This list of plants and their spacing requirements is designed to be a guide and nothing more. Rules are made to be broken, so plant your shrubs as close or far apart as you like. In fact, a closer spacing is desirable if you want fast coverage for an area; of course, with larger-growing shrubs this will require removing every other one once they begin to mature. Remember, a 1-gallon size shrub will eventually grow as large as the same species in a 5-gallon can.

Shrub	Spacing (trunk to trunk) In Feet
Abelia	3
Abelia Edward Goucher	2
Aucuba	
Bambusa	
Spreading Bamboo	3
Falcata Bamboo	4
Berberis	
Japanese Barberry	2½
Mentor Barberry	2½
Purple-leaved Barberry	2
Wintergreen Barberry	3
Brunfelsia (Yesterday-Today-and-Tomorrow)	2½
Buxus (Boxwood)	2
Caesalpinia (Bird of Paradise)	3
Callicarpa (American Beautyberry)	3
Callistemon	
Bottlebrush	6-8
Weeping Bottlebrush	10
Calycanthus (Carolina Allspice)	3-4
Camellia	
Camellia Japonica (pruned for flowers)	3
Camellia Japonica (mature, fully grown plant)	8-12
Camellia Sasanqua	4-6
Carissa (Natal Plum)	2½
Cassia (Flowery Senna)	3-5
Cestrum (Night-scented Jasmine)	3
Chaenomeles (Flowering Quince)	2½

Shrub	Spacing (trunk to trunk) In Feet
Clethra	
Clethra Pringlei	3
Summer-sweet	4
Cocculus	3
Cortaderia (Pampas Grass)	3-4
Cotoneaster	
C. glaucophyllus	2-3
C. horizontalis	4
C. pannosus	2½
Duranta (Golden-dewdrop)	3-5
Elaeagnus (Silver Berry)	3-4
Euonymus	2
Fatsia	3-4
Feijoa (Pineapple Guava)	4-5
Gardenia	3
Dwarf Gardenia	2
Hibiscus (Rose-of-Sharon)	4
Hydrangea	
Common Hydrangea	2½
Oakleaf Hydrangea	3
Ilex	
American Holly	10-15
Aukberry	4-6
Chinese Holly	2-3
Dahoon Holly	4
English Holly	8
Ilex Rotunda	8-12
Possum Haw	4
Yaupon	5
Dwarf Yaupon	1½-2
Illicium (Star Purple Anise)	3-4
Itea (Sweetspire)	3
Jasminum	
Italian Jasmine	3-4
Primrose Jasmine	6
Juniperus (shrub)	2½-4
Lagerstroemia (Crapemyrtles)	3
Laurocerasus (Cherry Laurel)	4-6
Laurus (True Laurel)	4
Leucophyllum (Texas Purple Sage)	2½

Shrub	Spacing (trunk to trunk) In Feet
Leucothoe	2½-3
Ligustrum	
Wax-leaf Ligustrum	3-4
Glossy Privet	8-10
Spicebush	4
Lonicera japonica (Japanese Honeysuckle)	2½
Mahonia	
Leatherleaf Mahonia	2½
Burmese Mahonia	2½-3
Agarita Mahonia	3
Malpighia (Barbados Cherry)	2-3
Michelia (Banana Shrub)	6
Myrica (Southern Waxmyrtle	4-8
Myrtus	
Common Myrtle	2-3
Dwarf Common Myrtle	1½-2
Nandina	2-3
Dwarf Nandina	1-2
Nerium (Oleander)	4-6
Dwarf Oleander	2-2½
Osmanthus	
Sweet Olive	6
Osmanthus fortunei	6-8
Philadelphus (Mock Orange)	3
Photinia (Fraser's Photinia)	4
Pittosporum	4
Variegated Pittosporum	3
Wheeler's Pittosporum	2½
Podocarpus (Japanese Yew)	3
Poncirus (Trifoliate Orange)	2-4
Punica (Pomegranate)	4-6
Dwarf Pomegranate	2
Pyracantha (Fire Thorn)	4
Raphiolepis (Indian Hawthorn)	2½
Rhamnus (Carolina Buckthorn)	6-8
Rhododendron (Azaleas)	3-4
Dwarf Azaleas	2-2½

	Spacing (trunk to trunk) In Feet
Rhus (Flameleaf Sumac)	4
Sophora (Mescal Bean)	8
Ternstroemia (Cleyera)	3
Viburnum	
Arrowwood Viburnum	3
Japanese Viburnum	4
Black Alder or Possum Haw Viburnum	3-4
Sandankwa Viburnum	3
Roundleaf Viburnum	3
Xylosma	4-6

Vine	Spacing (trunk to trunk) In Feet
Antigonon (Coral Vine)	12
Asarina (Snapdragon Vine)	2
Bignonia (Cross Vine)	8
Bougainvillea	4
Campsis (Trumpet Creeper)	12
Texas Clematis	3
Clytostoma (Argentine Trumpet Vine)	8
Decumaria (Climbing Hydrangea)	15
Dioscorea (Potato Vine)	4-6
Fatshedera	3
Ficus (Climbing Fig)	4
Gelsemium (Carolina Jessamine)	3-4
Hedera (Ivies)	2-3
Lonicera (Trumpet Honeysuckle)	4
Macfadyena (Cat's-Claw Funnel Creeper)	15-25
Passiflora (Passionflower)	4
Stigmaphyllon (Butterfly Vine)	4-6
Trachelospermum jasminoïdes (Confederate Jasmine)	3-4
Vitis (Muscadine, Grape)	12
Wisteria	15-20

Index

Index to Botanical Names

Shrubs

Abelia x grandiflora, 17
Aucuba japonica, 18

Bambusa glaucescens (Multiplex), 18
Berberis Thunbergii, 19
Brunfelsia pauciflora, 19
Buddleia Danidii, 59
Buxus sempervirens, 20

Caesalpinia gilliesii, 20
Callicarpa americana, 20
Callistemon citrinus (lanceolatus), 20-21
Calycanthus floridus, 21
Camellia japonica, 21-24
Carissa grandiflora, 24
Cassia corymbosa, 25
Cestrum nocturnum, 25
Chaenomeles speciosa, 25-26
Clethra alnifolia, 26
Cocculus laurifolius, 26
Condalia hookeri, 59
Cortaderia selloana, 26-27
Cotoneaster species, 27
Cyrilla racemiflora, 59

Duranta repens, 27

Elaeagnus pungens, 27
Euonymus americana, 27-28
Exochorda, 59
Eysenhardtia texana, 59

Fatsia japonica, 28
Feijoa sellowiana, 28-29
Forsythia, 59

Gardenia jasminoides, 29

Hamamelis virginiana, 59
Hibiscus syriacus, 29
Hydrangea quercifolia, 29-30

Ilex aquifolium, 32
Ilex cassine, 30-31

Ilex cornuta, 31
Ilex crenata, 31
Ilex decidua, 31-32
Ilex glabra, 32
Ilex opaca, 32
Ilex rotunda, 32
Ilex vomitoria, 32
Illicium floridanum, 32-33
Itea virginica, 33

Jasminum humile, 33
Jasminum mesnyi, 33
Juniperus, 59-60

Lagerstroemia indica, 33-34
Laurus nobilis, 34-35
Leitneria floridana, 60
Leucophyllum frutescens, 35
Leucothoe populifolia, 35
Ligustrum japonicum, 35-36
Ligustrum lucidum, 36
Lindera benzoin, 36
Litsea aestivalis, 60
Lonicera japonica, 38
Loropetalum chinense, 60

Mahonia bealei, 38-39
Mahonia lomariifolia, 39
Mahonia trifoliolata (Berberis), 39
Malpighia glabra, 39
Michelia Figo (fuscata), 40
Myrica cerifera, 40
Myrtus communis, 40-41

Nandina domestica, 41
Nerium oleander, 41-42

Osmanthus fragrans, 42

Philadelphus x virginalis, 42
Photinia x Fraseri, 42-43
Pieris, 60
Pittosporum Tobira, 43
Podocarpus macrophyllus, 44
Poncirus trifoliata, 44
Prunus caroliniana, 44

Punica Granatum, 44-45
Pyracantha Koidzumii, 45

Raphiolepis indica, 45-46
Rhamnus caroliniana, 46
Rhododendron, 46-48
Rhus copallina, 48
Rosa laevigata, 60

Sophora secundiflora, 48-49
Spiraea, 60-61
Styrax, 61

Taxus, 61
Ternstroemia gymnanthera, 49

Vaccinium arboreum, 61
Viburnum dentatum, 49
Viburnum japonicum, 49
Viburnum nudum, 49-50
Viburnum suspensum, 50
Viburnum Tinus (Laurustinus), 50

Weigela, 62

Xanthoceras sorbifolium, 62
Xanthorhiza simplicissima, 62
Xylosma congestum (senticosa), 50

Zanthoxylum Fagara, 62

Vines

Antigonon leptopus, 51
Asarina (Maurandya) antirrhinifolia, 51

Bignonia capreolata, 51-52
Bougainvillea hybrida, 52

Calonyction aculeatum, 63
Campsis radicans, 52-53
Clematis texensis, 53
Clytostoma callistegioides, 53
Cocculus carolinus, 63

Decumaria barbara, 53-54
Dioscorea bulbifera, 54

Ficus pumila, 54

Gelsemium sempervirens, 54-55

Hedera canariensis, 55

Ipomoea spp., 63
Ipomoea alba, 63

Lonicera sempervirens, 55

Macfadyena (Doxanthus) Unguis-Cati, 56
Manettia cordifolia, 64

Parthenocissus quinquefolia, 64
Passiflora caerulea, 56

Smilax lanceolata, 64
Stigmaphyllon ciliatum, 56-57

Thunbergia grandiflora, 64
Trachelospermum jasminoides, 57

Vitis rotundifolia, 57-58

Wisteria sinensis, 58

Index to Common Names

Shrubs

Agarita, 39
Althaea, 29
American
   Beautyberry, 20
   Holly, 32
Anise (Star Purple, Florida), 32-33
Aralia, Japanese, 28
Arrowwood Viburnum, 49
Aucuba, 18
Azalea, 16, 46-48

Bamboo, 18-19
   Heavenly, 41
Banana Shrub, 40
Barbados Cherry, 39
Barberry, 19
Bay Laurel, 34-35
Bird of Paradise, 20
Black Alder, 49-50
Bottlebrush, 20-21
Boxwood, 15, 20
Burford Holly, 23
Butterfly Bush, 59

Camellia, 21-24
Cape Jasmine, 29
Carolina
   Allspice, 21
   Buckthorn, 46
Cedar, 59-60
Ceniza, 35
Cherokee Rose, 60
Cherry Laurel, 44
Chinese
   Holly, 31
   Witch Hazel, 60
Cotoneaster, 27
Corkwood, 60
Crapemyrtle, Dwarf, 33-34
Crimson Bottlebrush, 20-21

Dahoon Holly, 30-31
Deciduous Holly, 31-32
Dwarf Crapemyrtle, 33-34

Elaeagnus, Thorny, 27
English Holly, 32

Farkleberry, 61
Fatsia, Japanese, 28
Fire Thorn, 45
Flameleaf sumac, 48
Florida
   Anise, 32-33
   Leucothoe, 35
Flowering Quince, 25-26
Flowery senna, 25
Fraser's Photinia, 42-43
French Mulberry, 20

Gallberry, 32
Gardenia, 29
Glossy Abelia, 17-18
Glossy Privet, 36
Golden-Bells, 59
Golden-dewdrop, 27
Gold-dust Aucuba, 18

Heavenly Bamboo, 41
Holly
   American, 32
   Chinese, 31
   Dahoon, 30-31
   English, 32
   Inkberry, 32
   Japanese, 31
   Possum Haw, 31-32
   Yaupon, 32
Honeysuckle, Japanese, 38
Hydrangea, Oakleaf, 29-30

Indian Hawthorn, 45-46
Inkberry, 32
Italian Jasmine, 33

Japanese
   Aralia, 28
   Aucuba, 18
   Barberry, 19
   Fatsia, 28
   Holly, 31

Honeysuckle, 38
   Viburnum, 49
   Yew, 44
Jasmine
   Cape, 29
   Italian, 33
   Night-Scented, 25
   Primrose, 33
Juniper, 59-60

Kidney Wood, 59

Laurel, 34-35
Leatherleaf Mahonia, 38-39
Leatherwood, 59
Lemon Bottlebrush, 20-21
Leucothoe, Florida, 35
Ligustrum, Wax-Leaf, 35-36
Lime Prickly Ash, 62

Mahonia, Leatherleaf, 38-39
   Burmese, 39
Mescal Bean Sophora, 48-49
Mock Orange, 42
Myrtle, 40-41

Natal Plum, 24
Night-Scented Jasmine, 25

Oakleaf Hydrangea, 29-30
Oleander, 41-42

Pampas Grass, 26-27
Paper Plant, 28
Pearlbush, 59
Photinia, 42-43
Pieris, 60
Pineapple Guava, 28-29
Pineapple Shrub, 21
Pittosporum, 15, 43
Pomegranate, 44-45
Pondspice, 60
Popcorn Shrub, 62
Possum Haw, 31-32
Possumhaw Viburnum, 49-50
Primrose Jasmine, 33

Vines

Subject Index

Peat moss, 9
pH, 8
Pine needles, 9
Pinkster Apples, 15
Planting, 6-7
Plastic, 9
Poodle shrubs, 12
Pruning, 2, 9-12

Rice hulls, 9
Roots, 6-7, 15

Saddleback caterpillar, 13, 15
Sandy soils, 7

Sawdust, 9
Screening, 3
Shrubs
    defined, 1
    vs. trees, 3
    uses for, 1-6
Soil, 4-5
Spacing, 17, 65-66
Spring color, 4
Starter solution, 8
Steiner solution, 8
Superphosphate, 8

Thinning, 9-11
Topiary, 11

Training, 9-12
Transplants, 6, 10
Trees
    vs. shrubs, 3

Vines
    uses of, 5

Whiteflies, 13-14
Wood chips, 9

Zinc, 16